MARITA

MARITA

*One Woman's Extraordinary Tale
of Love and Espionage
from Castro to Kennedy*

MARITA LORENZ

with
TED SCHWARZ

THUNDER'S MOUTH PRESS • NEW YORK

Copyright © 1993 Marita Lorenz
All rights reserved

First edition
First printing, 1993

Published by
Thunder's Mouth Press
632 Broadway, 7th Floor
New York, NY 10012

Library of Congress Cataloging-in-Publication Data

Lorenz, Marita, 1939–
Marita: one woman's extraordinary tale of love and espionage from
Castro to Kennedy/Marita Lorenz, with Ted Schwarz.—1st ed.
p. cm.
Includes index.
ISBN 1-56025-055-0: $22.95
1. Espionage, American—Cuba.   2. United States—Foreign
relations—Cuba.   3. Cuba—Foreign relations—United States.
4. Castro, Fidel, 1927–   —Friends and associates.   5. Lorenz,
Marita, 1939–   . I. Schwarz, Ted.   II. Title.
E183.8.C9L66   1993
327.1273'07291—dc20   93-26239
                                      CIP

Printed in the United States of America

Distributed by
Publishers Group West
4065 Hollis Street
Emeryville, CA 94608
(800) 788-3123

DEDICATION

TO MY MOTHER: For your unending love, extraordinary courage, suffering, guidance, patience, and devotion.

TO MY FATHER: For your love, patience, wisdom, and teachings of navigation, foreign affairs, diplomacy, and for showing me the world.

TO MY DAUGHTER, MONICA: For saving my life—the love and happiness you give me, and for your courage during all those difficult days.

TO MY SON, MARK: For your loving devotion, bravery, care, companionship, and for saving my life so courageously.

TO MY SON, ANDRÉ: For your love, understanding, and for proving everybody wrong.

TO FIDEL AND MARCOS: Without whom this book would not have been possible.

TO ALEXANDER I. RORKE: Whose timely advice and sincere friendship prevented major disasters.

TO COL. "FRANCISCO QUESADA," a.k.a. "THE SWAMP FOX": Whose Carribean adventures provided the basis for many of our escapades.

TO "THE PROFESSOR": For his insight, prescience, wisdom, and for offering the means and sanctuary for more than one escape.

FOR SHELLY ABEND: For his loyalty and friendship with gratitude for fast action protection.

FOR SUSANA AND LINDA: My "sisters" always, whose love, understanding, and support sustained me many years and made this book possible.

TO OLIVER STONE: Whose faith, understanding, and patience provided me with direction, purpose, and support to finish this project.

TO JANET YANG: whose patience, loyalty, and faith in me are very much appreciated.

TO THE 23RD PCT. N.Y.P.D.: In gratitude for your rapid responses and personal concern.

TO SGT. HESS, 23RD PCT.: With deepest gratitude for your bravery in saving my daughter's life.

TO SENATOR HOWARD BAKER AND HOWARD LIEBENGOOD: For your courage, trust, and personal concern.

TO DAVE MCMICHAELS and all my brothers and sisters of A.N.S.A. (Association of National Security Alumni): For your courage, friendship, loyalty, and assistance.

TO MARY ANN AND "PAPA" AYVAZ, MY MANAGER: For your guidance, friendship, loyalty, and unselfish assistance in making this project possible.

TO BOB, DAVE, AND FRIENDS AT THE A.S.P.C.A. (American Society for the Prevention of Cruelty to Animals.)

TO DR. KASRIEL EILENDER: For the many years of wonderful care you gave me and my family.

TO DON, RALPH, AND FRANK OF STRASSWIMMERS PHARMACY: For your many years of care and friendship.

TO ALTON L. KIRKLAND: My husband of today.

TO LOUIS J. YURASITS: My husband of yesterday.

TO EDDIE FLYNN: a loyal friend who was forever there and like a second father to me.

Not forgetting the following special people in my life: Tom Guinzburg, Harvey Erikson, Francis X. Smith, Camilo Cienfuegos, Valerie Lorenz, Joe Lorenz, Philip Lorenz and my wonderful relations in Germany. Wayne Smith, Al "Ace" C. Lt. Enright, Frank L. and Frank O., Jim Rothstein, Bob Kelly, Dick Mantzer, Irwin C. Karden, George Santoni, Karen Flaherty, Jim Ridgeway.

TO MY ASSASSIN: For not going through with it.

I.M.L.

ACKNOWLEDGEMENTS

This book would not have gone to press without the many long, dedicated hours put into this project by Suzanne Ironbiter, editor; Schellie Hagan, fact checker and researcher; Stephanie Chernikowski, editorial covert operative.

I am especially grateful to my publisher Neil Ortenberg for making this project possible, and all employees at Thunder's Mouth Press who sifted through my various volumes of documents, not including my more personal albums that are still jealously guarded by F.C.

I.M.L.

CONTENTS

PRELUDE

The pills came from Chicago. There were two of them. White gelatin capsules. I thought I would have to break them, but the men from Chicago told me I wouldn't. They would dissolve completely and invisibly in any liquid, even water. There would be no odor, no color, no taste.

"Like a Mickey," one of them said, "only better. He won't be able to scream before he dies. It does something to the vocal chords. Paralyzes them. He won't make a sound."

There were two or three Mafia men with me in the Miami airport that day early in 1960. With them were leaders in Miami's exiled Cuban community, Alex Rorke and other officials from the CIA and the FBI, and Frank Fiorini a.k.a. Sturgis, a man who worked all sides. They were anxious, happy, congratulating themselves for the assassination I was about to accomplish.

The Mafia, intent on their interests in Miami and Havana, were convinced I would effectively use the poison capsules they provided. They had seen the *Confidential* magazine in which my mother told of my supposed kidnapping and rape, of the infant untimely ripped from my womb, then left bloody and mutilated on the bed in the Havana Hilton Hotel where I had been staying. To gain vengeance, they argued, I must return, take his life.

Fidel, his eyes, his face so clear, every detail—I dream of him still and when I do, he monopolizes my whole day. It is the hurt and frustration of a love half-finished or incomplete, begun when I was nineteen, marking my life now for thirty-four years. Within a year of that beginning, pain and anger crossed that love, and the forces of life and death cut me in two.

Covert CIA agents induced me to believe Fidel had left me to have my baby forced into birth and killed. They worked on me for three months. "Castro ruined you," they said. "You have the key to his suite. Put the pills in his milkshake. Mickey Finns—botulinum shellfish toxin—lethal within minutes. We'll be so proud of you. Your parents will burst with pride—such a patriotic assignment. And the money—God, Marita—you'll be set for life. We'll take care of that—open a bank account starting with two million dollars. An opportunity once in a lifetime. We don't usually use women in this field of covert assignments. But, then again, Marita, we feel you have what it takes . . . your background in Germany, Belsen . . . we know it all . . . know you are strong. History is in your hands."

I loved Fidel. My heart had a hole in the middle full of rage.

MARITA

I

THE
FIRST
ASSASSINATION

1

When my father's ship anchored in Havana, I savored the beat of mambo and rumba, the cocoa glacé ice creams served in a shell, the sweet scent of tropical jasmine. The beach sparkled like a field of tiny diamonds. The clear azure water, seemingly without depth, showed aquatic life further below the surface than any human could dive without special equipment.

My teenage home was the *M.S. Berlin*, the German luxury liner commanded by my father, Captain Heinrich F. Lorenz. It was anchored in Havana harbor on the afternoon of February 27, 1959. It was the last stop of our yearly two-month cruise to the West Indies.

I was nineteen and a half. Soon my sea days, my devil-tomboy days, would be no more. Since my mother had begun doing intelligence work for the National Security Agency and was away on assignments, I had sailed the world with my father. Even when I wasn't supposed to, I'd sneak on board as a stowaway. If I was caught and taken back to shore before the ship got out to sea, I would wait until they were too far out to turn back, sail myself alongside on a small craft, tie up to an emergency platform, and climb up.

My parents had enrolled me in the Merchants and Bankers Secretarial School in New York City and arranged for me to share our family apartment on West Eighty-seventh Street with my brother Joe, who worked for the United Nations. It would be the end of my pranks, of grabbing cold-cuts from the waiters carrying the passengers' buffet lunches, of sneaking into passengers' rooms and switching their shoes around, of diving overboard, of raiding the pantries and the kitchen with the aid of papa's master keys, of taking papa's pistol from the safe when he wasn't around and shooting it into the air, of playing with the crew as my family, of what was to me the best of every world—the freedom of the sea.

Instead of all that, I was to "learn a skill." Then I was to settle down to a proper marriage and family life, cooking, cleaning, rearing children for the young German doctor, son of I. G. Farben, to whom I was promised by my parents.

Earlier that morning, when Papa and I went ashore, I ate my last cocoa glacé and bought two colorful beaded bracelets, red and black, with "26 de Julio" sewn in the middle, and flags and banners celebrating "Fidel," "Revolucionario," and "Cuba Sí" from an old woman selling souvenir trinkets. On January 8, seven weeks before our arrival, Fidel Castro had ousted dictator Fulgencio Batista and entered Havana with his guerrilleros.

I was only vaguely aware of the dark side of Cuba—the prostitution, the lottery and gambling, the gangsters and graft, the rich against the poor. I didn't know then about organized crime figure Meyer Lansky and his friends Charles "Lucky" Luciano and Benjamin "Bugsy" Siegel, who dominated the Havana casinos, or his brother Jake, who handled the day-to-day management, or about syndicate members such as Carlos Marcello of New Orleans and Santo Trafficante, Jr., who let underlings, including a nightclub owner named Jack Ruby, run guns to whomever wanted them.

I didn't know that Joseph Kennedy would be rumored to have helped finance Castro, hoping to take control of the Havana nightlife and destroy Lansky's influence in Havana if Batista was defeated, because Kennedy had hated Lansky since bootlegging days of prohibition when they were rivals.

I didn't know about Teamsters Union leader Jimmy Hoffa and prominent Cleveland labor leader Bill Presser, who made money selling arms to both sides, or that Santo Trafficante, Jack Ruby, and Frank Fiorini/Sturgis were among the gun runners providing Fidel with weapons during his fight against Batista, or that all these men and others, like Sam Giancana of Chicago, just wanted the Havana nightclub scene to be business as usual after the revolution.

Shortly after noon, while I was standing at the railing of our ship in Havana harbor, there came into view a launch filled with more than twenty bearded men. They were carrying guns and wore bandoleers filled with ammunition. A commotion began among the passengers.

Papa was not to be disturbed from noon until three. He was napping to be alert for our midnight departure. Meanwhile the launch was approaching and some of the passengers were terrified, convinced they were about to be taken over.

One of the stewards, probably assuming I would wake Papa, asked me to intervene. Fancying myself the master of the ship when Papa was not available, I went up to the top deck, from which I could best see our unexpected visitors.

I gave my usual shrill, unladylike whistle. This startled the soldiers. One, standing taller than the rest, lost his balance. His rifle fell on the launch deck with a clank. The launch backed away about two feet as the man looked up towards me before almost falling into the choppy sea. For a second or two, our eyes met. Then his cap flew off into the sea, and I could see him hanging on for dear life, not giving up the safety of his launch with his feet or the landing deck with his hands.

I couldn't help laughing, though I covered my mouth in embarrassment. To make it good, I called down, *"Esperarte un momento!"* The ship's officers waved me to come down.

The tropical wind hit me as I stepped out onto the top of the landing platform. Staring down, I again met the eyes of the taller soldier. He stood, swaying, at the bottom of the steps, looking up at me. He stared at me, not knowing what to say, and I stared back.

He took the first step upwards, which was my cue to go downward. Step by step, I tried to compose myself. Coming closer, all watching, we met right in the middle of the swaying gangplank alongside of our massive ship. The wind mixed with free-flowing sea spray trying its best to dislodge us both. I would not and could not let him pass on the narrow one-person-only stairs.

In the middle, as we faced each other determinedly in a stalemate, he stated cautiously to me in broken English, "I, my name is Dr. Castro, Fidel. Please. I—can I please come to visit your great ship? I . . . I . . . I am Cuba! You is *Alemán?*"

I responded in Spanish without accent, but not put together correctly. "My name is Ilona Lorenz. I am German. I represent the commander and this vessel, which is Germany you are now stepping on. Can I help you? Please, no need for this!" I put out my hand for his rifle. I was above all determined that no weapons were to go aboard.

He put his head sideways to look at his hand holding the rifle. To break the ice, before he lost his patience, I said, "Germany is at peace with Cuba. I'll take the rifle. Otherwise, you're not coming on board."

His look of trying to size me up turned to a smile as he

handed me the rifle. Our hands touched for a second. His pleading eyes and eagerness made me feel sorry for him. Since he surrendered his rifle to me, I nodded okay, though not forgetting that he had a .45 caliber revolver on his left hip and could easily have put it to my back. The passengers above clapped.

Walking up the stairs, I thought of his eyes, his height, his smile. I liked him, this tall rebel soldier. I also told myself that, as soon as we were on board, his .45 was going to go.

One by one, following him, twenty-five soldiers came aboard. They included his closest associates of the revolution— Celia Sanchez, Camilo Cienfuegos, and his naval attaché, Capitan Fernandez. Fidel, staying by my side, looked up and around like a tourist in awe.

I said, "Now you take off that gun too and have everyone put all arms down here on the floor. Please!"

Fidel ordered his grumbling men to disarm, and an arsenal of weapons piled up on the floor. "They will be guarded. You'll get them back," I assured him.

He said that he had been studying our ship from the balcony of his headquarters on the twenty-third floor of the Havana Hilton Hotel. Never having been on an ocean-going vessel, he decided to take some of his friends and come out for a tour.

Fidel asked repeatedly for the captain. I said he was temporarily indisposed and that I was in charge until three P.M. I felt proud and confident performing my duty, never afraid for a moment, yet his presence made me nervous. His piercing eyes, his smile, his physical attraction put my totally unguarded emotions in turmoil. I chose stupid words. I was childish. My eyes met his and then dropped to his combat boots with one lace untied, his two different socks, the four cigars in his left fatigue pocket, his solid hands, white skin, black curls, gold crucifix on a gold chain, his height (six-foot-three, almost a foot taller than I am).

Having disarmed this group of so-called deadly revolutionaries so that they could not take over my ship, what next? Guide a tour while Papa slept—but where to start? I decided on the engine room. As we waited for the elevator, Fidel, cigar in mouth, dropped ashes on the oriental rug and then put his boot over the ashes and apologized.

The ride down was silent. Fidel's eyes were on mine, his body right next to mine, his breath and beard brushing my nose, his hand holding me protectively around the waist. I was still clutching his confiscated rifle; the barrel was between his legs. If I had accidentally pulled the trigger, I would have blown, at that moment, Cuba's leader's vital private parts all over "German soil."

When the never-ending elevator ride jerked to a stop, I let myself fall against him. He hugged me, pulling me towards him, the rifle and my hand almost between his uniformed pants legs. I leaned willingly towards him, embarrassed so very much, but liking it also so very much. Never having kissed anybody, never having had a boyfriend, experiencing my first physical attraction to a man so wrong and yet so right, I wanted to keep this feeling forever. I wanted to hug and never let go. And yet, who was this soldier matching wits with me? How dare he come so close? How dare he change me? It did not seem possible that everything could change in so little time.

The door opened and I held my hand out to his to lead him down the oily steps into the noisy engine room. His men followed us on to the tall grated steel walkway. We looked down upon the suggestive pistons, huge and loud, Fidel and all his men amazed, drunk on German technology.

Still holding my hand, Fidel stared at me and eagerly tried to tell me, over the din, about himself and Cuba. He stroked my braids and smiled. Then he moved away to explain the engine room to his men. I began to contrive how to lose the tailing army so he and I could be alone. At the same time, I wanted my uncontrollable desires to go away.

We had about forty minutes before Papa would surface. I suggested cold German beer, and led the soldiers to the bar. It was dark, with candles lit on each table. Cuban mambo music was playing. I ordered Beck's Bremen bottled beer for all, on my tab, which was nonexistent. Drinking the beer from the bottle, Fidel said, "It's good. Everything in *Alemania* is good!" Trying to act grown-up, I ordered for myself a Cuba Libre (rum and coke) and told the waiter not to tell Papa. We all held up our drinks and toasted, "Salud!"

"Cuba Libre!" Fidel said.

"Alemania Siempre," I responded.

Fidel reached his left hand under the table, on top of my hand, which was still holding his confiscated rifle. I opened my knees, let the rifle fall to the floor, and studied his reaction. He smiled, but was serious. His hand squeezed mine. I was in over my head. I had bats and butterflies in my stomach. I loved everything about him. I was terribly nervous at his glances and fixed, serious stares into my eyes.

We talked about the ship, about Cuba and Germany. When I asked him what time it was, he brought his left arm towards me to show me. He had two wristwatches, one face up, one down. When I asked him why he wore two watches, he said, "One for yesterday and one for the time I never have enough of."

The first officer and the chief engineer, having got wind that I was with Fidel Castro and his army in the bar (off-limits to me), barged in. I took that as my excuse to go to my stateroom, put down my tomboy pigtails, and change into a dress for afternoon coffee time.

9

I rejoined the group on the veranda, top deck. They were heading slowly towards the bridge, to my father. The first officer fell back, leaving me to do the introductions. By then the ship photographer had caught us and started taking pictures of us everywhere.

Papa was wearing his elegant white uniform, its gold braids, buttons, and insignia glistening in the sun. Seeing me and my army below, he bellowed, *"Was ist denn das?"* (What is this?).

The gold chain leading to the outer bridge, where Papa was king, had a large sign stating VERBOTEN (forbidden). This whole scene was *verboten*.

I said, "This is Dr. Fidel Castro Ruz, the commander of Cuba. He wishes to see the ship. He'll depart again before we sail. He wants to meet you."

Papa, the diplomat's diplomat, switched to speaking Spanish as he politely greeted Fidel. He had the chief steward bring a silver tray with sandwiches, cakes, coffee, and drinks. He showed Fidel and his men through the bridge, the chart room, the wheel room, and led them to his cabin. Fidel praised the luxury and magnificence of the *M.S. Berlin*.

Appropriate to nothing, Fidel commented, "Your daughter, she is very knowledgeable."

Papa cut him short, saying, "Yes, sometimes too much so. She thinks she could be captain of the ship."

Fidel smiled and said, "I think she could be."

Papa grunted, reluctantly adding, "Yes, she is knowledgeable. She has been sailing with me for many years."

As the men talked and drank, they became friendlier towards one another. At one point Fidel grew somewhat solemn, looking at my father like an older mentor and confiding, "Captain, I am Cuba now. I successfully led my revolution down from the mountains, and now I have a lot to learn about politics. I have to keep my promises to my people and undo what Batista has done."

My father said, "The one thing you must never do is alienate the United States in any way."

"No," said Fidel. "I have no intention of doing that. None. In fact, I want to have a meeting with the United States." He furiously denied any association with Communism. He called his revolution Humanism.

The men talked and drank for three hours. Fidel was interested in technology, economics, trade, and tourist dealings with West Germany. He asked my father to stay in Cuba and become his Ambassador of Tourism, with an office, cars, and staff in the Presidential Palace next door to his. My father was flattered and thanked Fidel, but he explained that he had an obligation to his company and his country.

At six P.M. sharp, Papa invited Fidel and all his men to the captain's table in the first class dining room for supper. I sat next to Fidel, who sat next to Papa. Fidel wrote me a note on a napkin: *"Para Marita, Alemanita Mia—Siempre, Fidel, Feb. 27, 1959."* He folded it and gave it to me under the table.

After dinner, we all went to the lounge. Fidel seriously and politely asked Papa if I could return to Cuba as his personal secretary to translate letters for him. Papa was floored and shocked. I blushed purple and giggled. Fidel promised he would get me an office and a guard, and I would be absolutely safe. Papa diplomatically stuttered, "Your offer, Dr. Castro, is too kind, but not at all possible. She must go to school in New York. She's but a child."

Papa excused himself to go to the bridge. Sailing time at midnight was in a few hours.

As the tropical sunset fell, colored dancing lights decorated the ship's outlines. The warm tropical breeze carried a scent of jasmine and the sounds of rumba music from the aft deck. Fidel and I walked in the company of his men and two ship's officers. He took my hand. Pretending to show him the magnificent view of Havana harbor, I pulled him quickly in between lifeboats six and seven. The others kept walking.

Fidel turned me towards him and held me tightly, rocking back and forth, his body against mine, my arms embracing his solid back, my sleeve getting caught on his gun belt. I wanted never to let go of this moment. He held my face in his hands and kissed me—my first kiss—the aroma of his Cuban cigar on his beard. *"Dulce, te quiero, mi cielo,"* he whispered. His eyes were dark, sincere, gazing intensely into mine, his mouth and his kiss sweet and gentle on mine. "Be with me," he whispered.

"Oh Fidel, I can't. We sail in two hours."

"You no go, *Alemanita*."

"Yes, yes Fidel. I don't want to go, but I have to."

"You come to me, be with me, work with me for Cuba. I need you. I am Cuba. You will be Cuba with me."

"I'll come back."

"Am I too old for you? You're so young."

"You are fine, perfect."

He said he was thirty-three. I was nineteen.

I will never forget the words we spoke on that day, or the sweet love, the intense desire I had for him, or his desire for me.

An hour before sailing, we went up to the bridge so he and Papa could say farewell. Fidel had sent one of his men back to the island to get a bronze and gold plaque to give my father. Papa gave him gifts from the ship's stores. Knowing how much I liked cocoa glacé, Fidel had eight large cases delivered to the ship's freezer.

I took him to the sundeck above the captain's cabin, the bridge—the highest point of the ship after the crow's nest on the mast. Holding me, he pointed out the Havana Hilton, where he said he would be waiting for me. The view of Havana at dusk, in that moment with Fidel silently hugging me, was magnificent.

The engines began to hum. A deafening TOOT from the funnel behind us startled Fidel. It signaled all clear, farewell to Cuba. I led him down the steps to gather his men. The Cuban harbor pilot was already on board to guide us out of the harbor. In three days we would be in New York. Everything in me was changed.

Fidel took off one of his watches, the gold one, and put it on my wrist. *"Prometa,"* he whispered, "promise you will come back."

One by one, Fidel and his men picked up their rifles and arms and went down the gangplank. The signals announced departures, the anchor lifted. The launches bobbed out of view.

2

I was trying to settle down in New York, reading Herbert L. Matthew's article on Castro's Cuba in *The New York Times Magazine* and making Jell-O. I had been home for one day. My mother was on overseas assignment in Germany, my father en route back to Europe. The phone rang.

"Marita Lorenz?" asked the overseas operator.

"Yes," I said.

"One moment please, for the Prime Minister."

Shocked, I dropped the Jell-O all over my mother's new rug.

"I miss you," Fidel's hoarse, raspy voice came on the other end. "You come back?"

"I don't know. Papa sailed this morning. He'll be back in a month."

"Then you can come for one week. *Te quiero mucho, Alemanita.*"

Less than twenty-four hours later, three of Fidel's aides were at my door. They brought an official car to take me to his Cubana Airlines plane at Idlewild (now JFK) airport.

We had a large world map on our wall. I put a red circle around the island of Cuba and a pin in Havana.

Nervous, having anxiety attacks, filled with pangs of guilt, shy, overwhelmed, scared, happy, excited, I tried to look businesslike.

My three escorts treated me seriously, even royally. As if in a dream, I was transported from 344 West Eighty-seventh Street to the Havana Hilton, Suite 2406-8.

The room where Fidel lived was filled with lingering cigar smoke. It had a double bed, tropical decor and large mirrors. The closet was full of clean starched uniforms under plastic, caps, and boots. The dressers were littered with records, papers, money, scale tanks, Tonka toy tractors, and back hoes.

I went into the bathroom, washed and put on makeup. After an hour, Fidel's key turned in the door. When he saw me, he quickly put out his cigar in an ashtray and grabbed me, picking me clear up off the floor. He swung me around, hugging and holding me. We rocked back and forth. As he kissed me, I held him tightly. It did not seem possible to feel so warm, so wonderfully in love, so secure. He asked me to be with him forever, and I said, "Yes, always, always, always."

Our passion had no thought for the world around us. Together, hand in hand, we closed the curtains. He hung his gun belt over the lamp. He gave orders over the phone to Celia Sanchez and Che Guevara not to bother him. We put his favorite Cuban music on the record player and set it on automatic. I was never so joyous or so nervous.

I remember every detail of that first day with my first love— his body next to mine, our clothes slowly shed, desire taking over, our fitting perfectly, our shared desire that seemed only death could terminate. We cuddled, romped, played, whispered tender words, made love again and again. I wept childish tears

1 5

of joy, guilt, ecstasy. We were in bliss for five hours. I watched him sleep, his white skin, black curly hair. We took a long shower together, drowning together.

"You don't seem completely undressed," I said. "You still wear the beard."

THE FIRST ASSASSINATION

3

A persistent knock on the door was followed by a demanding voice. Raúl, Fidel's brother, said there were affairs of state that urgently needed to be attended to. Fidel got dressed. "I'll be back," he said. "I love you. Order room service. Don't go out."

"I'll wait," I said.

He went to "fix up Cuba."

The next day I awoke, set up my "office," sorted his mail, got jealous reading his fan letters from women, made myself pretty, waited. I felt guilty. I wrote my mother that I was seeing family friends in Cuba and helping Fidel with his correspondence.

I trusted Fidel. There was loyalty, trust, respect in my love for him. There was also longing, waiting, pain. I wanted him to be proud of me. I was accepted and greeted by Celia, Camilio, and Che, and introduced to his personal guards, yet each day grew longer.

His hours were totally erratic. After a month, I was restless and tired of staying in the suite alone. To combat loneliness, I studied Spanish. With June Cobb I began translating his manifesto *History Will Absolve Me*, which he had written in prison under Batista.

Coming in one night at four A.M., he brought tropical orchids. He was in a loving mood. I threatened to leave. He threw a pillow at me, soothed me, pulled the sheet like a veil over my head. I wept with guilt and frustration. He put two large orchids on my sheeted head, grabbed some parsley from the cold cheeseburger tray and put it on top of the flowers.

"Don't move, my beloved," he said. "Now we marry!"

He knelt on the bed in front of me, made a cross with his hand, and said, "Now, do you, my *Alemanita,* Marita Lorenz want to marry with Fidel Castro?" He gently dried my tears.

"Yes," I said, "I do marry you, Fidel Castro, forever."

We laughed, hugged. He said he was Cuba, law, and God of all, including me, and so I was married in God's eyes.

"Yes, I know," he said, "you are alone too much. You are my wife now, and I will take you with me."

A week later, he gave me a diamond engagement ring with "*3/59, de Fidel para Marita, Siempre,*" engraved in the eighteen-karat gold setting.

4

Everyone knew I was Fidel's girlfriend. He provided me with my own honorary 26th of July uniform, issued me a .38 caliber revolver for a sidearm, and gave me the rank of Lieutenant. I had his personal letterhead for my secretarial duties. I was accepted by and blended with his closest people—his brother Raúl, Che Guevara, Ramiro Valdés, Camilo Cienfuegos, Celia Sánchez.

In April, I realized I was pregnant.

In mid-April, I accompanied Fidel and his aides on a fifteen-day visit to the United States—Washington, New York, Boston.

I felt nauseous, withdrawn.

Everybody in New York wanted a piece of him. As usual, I waited in the hotel suite. He returned ecstatic, elated from the attention given him. I moped. He viewed himself in the mirror. "I am like Jesus, don't you think? I have a beard, am thirty-three years old, and I am like God!"

Just pacify him, I thought. Dutifully but a little jealous, I untied his boots as he talked about the economic assistance he was sure to get.

"From whom?" I asked.

"Big brother," the USA.

He was gloating on his charisma with the beautiful female reporters at his press conference. I said, "Be careful. Your American brother doesn't understand your uniform, your beard, your guns, or your goals."

"But they love me, and I will help Cuba!"

Day by day, he was guided by his emotions, his dream of cleaning up and fixing Cuba. In Washington, it never occurred to him that President Eisenhower wasn't enthusiastically waiting for him to just drop by. He was shocked to discover the Comandante of Cuba had to give notice. Eventually he did see Vice President Nixon, but Nixon was barely polite to him— cool, cautious, instantly negative if not outright rude.

Fidel was deeply hurt. Despite what Nixon concluded, he was not a Communist at this time. He thought his revolution was for democracy in Cuba. Raúl and Che were strongly pro communist. Fidel's politics were those of pragmatism. Anything that would change the excesses of Batista and improve Cuba was fine with him.

The differences between Fidel and Raúl came out while we were in Washington being snubbed by the White House. Fidel felt close to the United States. He had spent time in New York and had even wanted to study there. But Raúl felt that Americans had been involved with the Batista corruption. He wanted to reject the American system of government since it had tolerated and supported Batista. Raúl constantly harped on the need to become a pure communist state. He pressed the idea day after day. If they were not together, Raúl would tell Fidel on the phone, "We'll get economic assistance elsewhere." Nixon's treatment pushed Fidel in Raúl's direction.

THE FIRST ASSASSINATION

Fidel said there was a man he needed to see before we left Washington. He said the man was tall, bearded, and did not dress well, much like himself. He could relate to that man, to his struggles, to the comments made against his physical appearance. To my surprise, we went to the Lincoln Memorial, and he stared at the statue.

The political tensions grew after we returned to Cuba. Fidel felt compelled to make changes as rapidly as possible, especially in the areas of education and medicine. Under Batista, there was no medical care for the poor, no education except for the elite. Raúl kept talking about Communism. Fidel tried his best, made mistakes, pushed on. His physical strength kept him going with little sleep.

5

Days would go by without my seeing him. I was always ready, always waiting. I stayed loyal, my diamond ring, the baby in my womb reassuring me.

During his absences, my insecure feelings ran wild. I had to share him with Cuba, and readily understood that. But I was not about to share him with other women. His mail was filled with fan letters and pictures of beautiful women wanting to meet him. What if he got some of his fan mail before I tore it up? What if there were notes quickly hand-delivered in the lobby, in the street? I worked myself up, pestered Celia, Raúl, Camilo.

I kept track of which foot had the black, which the blue sock, and checked with boxers he was wearing when he went out, but I never caught him.

Once, in my frustration, insecurity, and rage, in a frenzy of weeping, I took the bathers' elevator up and down four times looking for him. His *barbados* calmed me, escorted me back to my room. I thought Ava Gardner was after him; I had intercepted her many letters in which she expressed her desire to meet him.

I settled down to eat my room service cheeseburger, milkshake, and cocoa glacé after I pinned the fly on his boxer shorts together with safety pins, tied the leather laces on his boots together in a tight knot, and put all his Tonka trucks, tanks, and tractors upside down. I blasted his favorite record, *"Piano Majico,"* until Che banged on the adjoining wall to our suite. Then I cried myself to sleep.

The next morning I realized how immature and stupid I'd been. Che, Camilo, Celia all insisted he was busy. My head down, ashamed, I cried, "Just tell me I have not been replaced." Camilio hugged me like a brother, dried my tears, and reassured me.

Still, I continued to open the door and look down the hall twenty times a day. In my solitude, I recalled his words and instructions, digging deeper into Cuba's problems. One day I looked in the mirror at my self-pitying, stupid, pregnant self and decided I needed to get out more.

The lobby of the hotel was packed full of people pushing and clamoring to see Fidel. Some of the people tried to talk to me, to hand me notes. As I retreated from the crush, clinging to my guards, a drunken middle-aged woman staggered into the elevator with us.

"So you're the little bitch who's hiding Fidel!" she slurred. She introduced herself as Ava Gardner, and slapped my face hard. Captain Pupo, one of Fidel's guards pulled his gun.

I learned my lesson to stay in my room, wait, study, and obey. For the first time, I understood what Fidel was up against, why he needed ten agents and a staff of one hundred just to book his appointments. I decided to pull myself together. I translated more letters and organized his files.

That night Fidel told me he had fixed up Ava Gardner with an aide, who was to satisfy her in a suite at the National Hotel, compliments of Cuba.

6

In late August, visibly pregnant, my 26th of July uniform blouse hanging loose, I went with Fidel, Raúl, Camilo, and about fifty uniformed men to act as their translator; they were going to "oversee" the gambling operations in the luxury hotels. Raúl had decided to rid Cuba of U.S. gambling interests. Fidel said he was not opposed to gambling but to the vice and corruption that went with it.

At the Havana Riviera, a middle-aged, rather pleasant American gentleman by the name of Colonel Charlie Baron was in charge of the gaming tables and hotels. Raúl ordered his men to confiscate all of the slot machines and overturn the green felt crap tables and roulette wheels without destroying anything.

The casino workers were concerned, but were promised other work. Colonel Baron pleaded. Raúl was adamant. The *barbados* pulled back the long red drapes and opened the windows. The crystal chandelier swayed as the breeze mixed with the stale smells of liquor and cigarette smoke.

I was standing in the Riviera lobby when a square-faced

man in a Cuban uniform slithered up next to me. This unknown individual said to me in perfect American English, "He's making a big mistake." I said nothing, but a chill went through me. This individual had approached me once before, in the lobby of the Hilton coffee shop, where he wrote me a note on a place mat: "I can help you, Marita." That time my guards interfered. Now I was alone. I was leary of his icy, shifty eyes and the disdainful way he looked me slowly up and down. I was confused about his purpose in targeting just me.

"Are you okay?" he asked contemptuously.

None of Castro's men would ask that.

"Look," I said, "I don't know who you are, but I don't need any help."

From Captain Pupo I caught the name of the "Americano," Frank Fiorini. "He's bothering me. What does he want? I don't trust him," I told one of the men. Ramiro Valdés approached Fiorini. He left. Later that day I saw him talking to Jesús Yanes Pelletier, Fidel's aide.

I returned to our suite. I felt an unknown deep uneasiness. I was unsure what to make of the mysterious Fiorini or whether to tell Fidel, Raúl, Camilo, or just to forget about it.

Celia found out about the confiscations and that in the raid, several of the operators had been arrested and jailed. It wasn't certain what Raúl wanted to do with them. They included Jake Lansky, Santo Trafficante, and Carlos Marcello. When she couldn't find Fidel, she asked me what to do.

I considered that Papa told Fidel not to alienate the United States. Locking up Americans didn't seem like a smart move.

I took four of the sheets of stationary Fidel had signed and given me, filled in one name per sheet, adding my version of an "official" order to release them. I did it in front of Castro's aide Pelletier, and told him to release them. Pelletier was afraid I was doing the wrong thing, and he would pay the price. I said I was doing what Castro wanted.

We drove to the prison. I asked each man in turn if he had killed someone, and each said he had not. They were confused by my uniform, by the fact that I spoke English without an accent, and was an American citizen wearing a Lieutenant's uniform. I said they were free to go. One of them thanked me profusely.

"Lady," he said, "I'll never be able to thank you enough. Do you know who I am?"

Only much later did I learn of the convoluted personal manipulations, politics, organized crime factions, and CIA involvement in all of this.

Fidel was annoyed when he found out. "You don't want to lock up any Americans," I told him. "Remember what Papa said. Don't upset the Americans. Gambling isn't bad. They didn't kill anybody."

He laughed, then agreed. He didn't even know they had been locked up.

I also intervened when Raúl wanted to destroy the confiscated slot machines and gaming tables. I convinced him to store everything. Today everything is still warehoused, dusty and outdated.

My actions had created two impressions of me in the minds of the gambling Dons. They felt they owed me a favor and that I knew this. They also assumed I knew who they were and what they represented. They probably thought that, when I ordered them freed without Fidel's immediate knowledge, I had taken a stand in support of organized criminals and could be trusted. They thought I could be brought into the nastier aspects of their world without risk of my revealing what they said or did.

7

Everything began to fall apart for me in October. Raúl had been confiscating properties and working on agrarian reforms. Pro-Batista people were going to Miami, then returning to clean out dirty money in banks. They were backed by the CIA, hired to commit covert actions against Fidel.

Nixon, with the approval of President Eisenhower, was actively working to help coordinate covert strikes against Cuba. Nixon was close to the anti-Castro movement in Miami. He refused to engage in dialogue with Cuba—an uninformed and negative decision which sealed Fidel's and Cuba's fate to this day.

When I first heard the sounds of the bombs from an aircraft attack on a sugar plantation on the outskirts of Havana, I thought the explosions were fireworks. Fidel later had to explain to me what was going on. He was tipped off that these raids were directed by anti-Castro forces in Miami.

My continued stay in Cuba had upset my family. My brother sent a friend of his, a United Arab Republic diplomat who was also at the United Nations, to check on my well-being and convince me to return home. Fidel, jealous and outraged, physically expelled the man from his room and had him driven to the airport in his pajamas. Having seen me, Sayeed reported to my brother I was obviously near to giving birth.

I had no idea that my staying in Cuba might endanger my life. Havana was still a popular place for tourists to visit, a tropical paradise to international travelers. Professional baseball players were visiting the island. Members of the American Society of Travel Agents were enjoying the hospitality of the Hilton.

On October 15th, Fidel was away working in another province of the island. The birth of our child was predicted for the beginning of December.

I had gotten into the habit of ordering room service instead of going to one of the hotel's restaurants. As I waited for the food, I remember glancing out the window of our hotel room and seeing the "Welcome ASTA" sign for the travel agents arriving at the Hilton. Then the meal came, including a glass of milk. Everything seemed normal, including the person who delivered my meal.

The drug was in the milk. I never tasted it, but I realized what was happening when it began to work. Suddenly I was tired, as though someone had dropped a blanket over my brain, dulling my thoughts, slowing my movements. I didn't have a sense of falling asleep. Instead, I knew that I was going to lose all consciousness. I felt I could not fight, nor could I think clearly enough to call for help or lock the room. For a moment I remembered the sign, remembered the milk. Then I knew nothing.

A cool, wet mist struck me in the face. I was in a car, the window partially open. We were driving along the *Malecón*—a popular scenic part of Havana where a wall kept high waves from sweeping across part of the winding streets. Someone was driving, and I heard a second person's voice. A man.

I slipped back into unconsciousness, never having gained enough strength to try to formulate words.

Someone was lifting me, talking in low tones. I was on a table, cold, probably metal. There was a needle in my arm, a pain, the sensation of an injection. I did not have the energy to cry out, but I could hear myself moaning.

Voices became clearer. Someone was arguing with another man, apparently a doctor. There was an argument. Someone, perhaps the doctor, said he didn't want to do it. He mentioned Fidel, spoke with fear about Fidel. There was a strong light. I lost consciousness.

At some point I awakened to find my stomach flattened, the baby gone. In the background I heard a baby crying. My baby. Alive . . . a clear cry.

Frightened, fighting total blackout, I called Fidel's name. He would protect the child, protect me.

A man appeared, apparently thinking I was still confused by the drugs. He said, "I'm Fidel." It was not Fidel.

It all made no sense. Confused, I became increasingly agitated as I fought to stay awake, to keep my life from falling into a dark tunnel.

Another injection, more hands lifting me. Again in the car. Again nothing.

When I awakened, I was back on the bed in my room. My head was clearer but my body was limp, leaden. I turned my head and could still see the "Welcome ASTA" sign. The travel agents were still enjoying beautiful Havana. My city. Fidel's Cuba.

The door opened, and this time I came to the fullest alertness I experienced since consuming the drugged milk. It was Camilo Cienfuegos. "My God, kid, what happened to you?" he asked, his voice indicating the horror of my condition. He was staring at my face, at the blood soaking my uniform pants. There were tears in his eyes, silent curses, deep concern.

I tried to indicate I needed water, but my mouth was too dry to speak. Later I would learn that it was a reaction to the drug given to me to induce labor that had been administered too rapidly for my safety. That was also the cause of my uncontrolled bleeding.

Camilo kneeled beside me, looked more closely at the stains, then got towels to pack me and stop the bleeding. He went to the bathroom for water, then got a straw so I could drink.

I was frightened. Each time he left the room, Camilo reassured me and locked the door. Each time he returned, silhouetted in the door with his beard, long hair, and the cowboy hat that he always wore, he looked like Christ.

I had blood poisoning, a raging fever, uncontrolled bleeding. Camilo had basic first-aid common sense. He brought antibiotics from a nearby hospital, helped me into clean clothes, brought me food, acted as my nurse, and stayed with me off and on.

He placed urgent calls to Fidel, who was still in the field. When he finally got through, I could hear Fidel screaming, "No, no, don't tell me this! Who?" I cried terribly at his anxiety.

Everything was in confusion. My mind kept returning to Fidel's instructions to completely avoid all counter revolutionaries. I was deeply depressed and changed inside. I wanted my mother, yet I was reluctant to leave. I tried to backtrack with Camilo, who said he knew what and why.

Camilo was worried about my bleeding and my being in

danger from Fidel's enemies. It seemed the only safe plan was for me to get medical attention outside of Cuba. He called my brother in New York and made arrangements for me to fly then return after being treated by my mother's doctor.

I insisted on wearing the bloody Lieutenant's uniform Camilo had removed from my body when trying to stop the hemorrhaging. The uniform was a symbol of my love and loyalty. It was a badge of honor against our enemies.

I was taken by Jeep to the airport. On my finger was my engraved engagement ring, in my pockets were a key to our suite and Fidel's love letters. There was no question in my mind that I would be back soon.

8

My mother, accompanied by four U.S. government officials, met me at the airport. The officials got in the car with us. They never left us. They came with us to our apartment.

I wanted to talk to my mother alone, but that was difficult. The agents watched every move I made. They said I was in "protective custody." I felt like I was a criminal. Defiant, deflated, depressed, rebellious, exhausted, weak, helpless, I stared sullenly at the agents, then cried like a child in my mother's arms.

During my childhood, Mama and I comforted one another after we suffered under the Nazis in World War II. She comforted me then, at the end of the war, when I was raped by a Sergeant in the occupying American army. I was seven then. The experience of abuse to my body made part of me withdraw. I was numb. I became quiet. I endured life.

My mother could do nothing to stop the plan, full of cunning and manipulation, her colleagues, the intelligence officials, had for me—a plan that used her well.

* * *

I was born a few weeks before Hitler invaded Poland. It was August 18, 1939. My twin sister Ilona was killed early in the war by a Polish displaced person. My parents, grief stricken, added her name to mine. Papa called me Ilona. Mama called me Marita.

My mother was an American citizen, Alice June Lofland, from a wealthy Virginia family, a cousin of Henry Cabot Lodge. She had led a life of glamor, privilege, and romance as an actress and dancer. In 1932 when she was traveling by boat to Paris for a role in one of the first talking films, her beauty caught the attention of the ship's Captain Heinrich Friedrich Lorenz. He fell in love instantly and sent her letters and flowers wherever she traveled. He was sixteen years her senior. She married him and settled down to raising a family in Bremerhaven, the company town of his employer, the Lloyd Lines, and later in Bremen. After a year, Mama gave birth to triplets, only one of whom survived. He was my brother Joe (Joachim). Then came Philip, after that my sister Valerie, then Ilona and I.

When the war began, Papa had to leave the luxury liner business and became a captain in the Navy. He did not defect because, like many men who hated Hitler, he was a loyal German who was willing to ensure personal Hell if his country could eventually return to normal. The Nazi government would have allowed my mother to return alone to the United States, but she would have to abandon her children in Germany. We children were assured lives of privilege in Germany because of my father's respected status, but Mama wouldn't leave us.

Papa had a close and personal association with Admiral Wilhelm Canaris. During the early war years, he, Canaris, and other German officials held clandestine Resistance meetings in our home in Bremen. He introduced Mama into the world of espionage, and both my parents became double, even triple agents.

MARITA

From 1941 to 1945 we did not see Papa, and he was unaware of events transpiring on the home front with Mama and us four children. His activities at sea included overseeing and managing German naval supply units, and nautical management of weatherships and stations in the Arctic. His weathership was torpedoed by British bombers on May 2, 1943, and surviving personnel were taken prisoner. He and the officers were transferred to a British vessel, then to a POW camp in England. During processing, several "undocumented individuals," among them a family with infants and children, were discovered. The men were disguised as fishermen and smelled of herring.

The winters in Bremen, where we lived during the war, were intensely harsh. There was no coal prepared for home use. Instead, Mama and the other women had to chop massive lumps into burnable pieces. Although the coal was relatively soft, the splinters cut like tiny knives, and the women had sore hands, soot in their hair, and bleeding sores on their faces.

Soap was so scarce that clothes had to be boiled for cleanliness, then hung in the garden to dry. The garden was also where a fire was kept burning for heat and cooking, and where Mama had to dig to find ground water when the plumbing was turned off.

Our diet consisted of black bread, turnips, cabbage, peas, dried beans, and lentils, with fruit from trees and bushes that survived nearby bombings. Gas and electricity still worked, but only for three hours a day. Such commodities as toilet paper, coffee, tea, and rice were non-existent.

Bombs fell in the area. Machine gun fire and small arms bullets flew, and tanks rumbled in the distance. Soldiers were in the meadows. I was provided with a small cooking pot which was to be kept on my head at all times to protect me from shrapnel and other debris.

Our cellar was reinforced and turned into our primary living quarters. I was always with Mama, but the older children were sometimes scattered among friends. Philip stayed with a woman who had a grand piano in her living room. The piano was a delight for my brother when he was allowed to play it, and when he slept, fearful of bombs crashing, he curled up underneath the instrument. Later he joked that sleeping under the piano helped make him the world class concert pianist he became.

Mama knew how dangerous the air raids could be, and when the house was at risk, we'd race to the nearest air raid shelter. I still have memories of the sights and sounds of a city under attack. The approaching planes sounded like droning thunder, the noise growing ever louder as they flew closer. You could time the moment of the attack by listening to the pitch of their approaching engines.

Then there would be the whistles of the bombs dropping. While the explosions were frightening, what remains in my memory are the smells. If I close my eyes, I can still recall the aroma of white hot phosphorous and burning wood t. · filled the air when a target was being destroyed.

No one was certain whether or not to trust Mama. She was not German, and that made her suspect. But she was a mother, and her children were being raised as Germans, a fact important to Hitler's effort to increase the youth for the "triumphant" new Reich. And she was married to a German hero. As a result, she was alternately treated with great respect, left alone to survive as best she could with us, and imprisoned for interrogation for possible espionage. Her treatment depended upon the whims of the men in power, and the twists and turns of the war.

Mama engaged in espionage. Our cellar was rigged for both survival and for spying. A false wall hid radio equipment critical to the allies in occupied territory.

There is some confusion about what Mama did with the radio. On October 4, 1945, Mama received a letter from a man in Argenteuil, France, thanking her for her work. He was among the prisoners who were kept in small towns where they could be controlled without fear of escape. He had been able to sneak into our home periodically to use Mama's receiver to listen to the news coming from France. It was far more accurate than the reports issued by the German government, and he was able to spread reports to the Allied soldiers. The Gestapo would have killed all of us had they known, but the news, in addition to bringing comfort to the men, enabled them, at times, to coordinate espionage activities.

However, there was either more to the radio than the Frenchman knew or there was a second radio. I remember well how, every few days, Mama would go to the hidden radio area and remove either a telegrapher's key or a microphone. Sometimes she would tap out messages in Morse Code, and other times she would broadcast reports to the Allies. I knew that I was never to mention the radio, the hidden wall, or what Mama was doing.

We would periodically have high ranking German officers, "friends" of Papa, in our basement, and there were times Mama would stand or lean against the area where the radio was hidden. They never found the equipment.

Mama also acted as a supplier for the underground. When a fleeing prisoner of war needed civilian clothes and other items to pass safely through the streets, she provided them.

Many prisoners of war were engaged in forced labor throughout Bremen. They cleaned the debris, and did whatever tasks needed to be done. The increased freedom they enjoyed allowed them opportunities for espionage and escape. Many of the town's people hated them and acted as spies for the Gestapo to help keep the prisoners in line. A few, like my mother, used their limited freedom as a way of getting them help.

For example, Mama used to take whatever food we could

spare, wrap it in newspaper, then leave it on an ash pile. To the casual observer, she was placing trash in the wrong place, something that happened with enough frequency so that it did not seem out of the ordinary. The prisoners and displaced persons forced into labor knew to take the paper and open it when they could.

One of the neighbors, an ardent Nazi, community watchdog, and selfappointed spy caught my mother leaving food and denounced her to the National Socialist Party. The offense was a serious one, especially since many of the prisoners were deliberately being systematically worked to death through the issuance of limited provisions. Additional food either prevented or slowed their starvation, and thus was considered a minor form of treason. However, the actions did not endanger the ultimate victory of the Nazis, and since she was the wife of a high ranking Navy officer, Mama was just fined and severely warned against a repeat of her compassion.

Mama never stopped, though. She spotted a French prisoner of war working on the streets of Bremen. He was undernourished and ill-clothed, shivering as his body desperately tried to warm itself. More concerned with keeping the man alive than with her own safety, Mama openly gave him a hot bun to eat.

This time she received punishment. A Nazi soldier marched her through the streets of Bremen, prodding her with his bayonet. Where others could see, he kicked her with his heavy boots and slapped her in the face to show his contempt. Finally she was locked in a small basement room that was barren except for a pile of straw meant to serve as her bed. She was fed bread and water just adequate to sustain life. She was released not long afterward, apparently sufficiently punished.

As horrible as my mother's experience had been, it would have been worse had Papa not been so respected. Torture and release were signs of respect. Those of lesser importance would have been tortured to death.

Mama was subsequently watched by the Nazis. They could not understand what she was doing. Was she simply a "foolishly" caring non-Aryan with the "sense" to have married a good German man like Papa, or was she a spy? When my father's North German Lloyd Liner, the *Bremen,* which had been armed and camouflaged for an invasion of England was destroyed by fire while in port in March, 1941, Mama was a suspect. A fifteen-year-old seaman was blamed for carelessness. He was shot by the Gestapo. Many felt he was railroaded into a confession, and that there had been sabotage.

Fearing that it was only a matter of time before her spying led to something terrible happening to the family, Mama applied to the Swiss Consul for the chance to return to the United States. However, the war was too far along and her actions were no longer considered proper. The U.S. response to her plea was "get a divorce and leave your Nazi children in Germany." The Nazis arrested her on suspicion of espionage and passing information to the enemy.

The Gestapo arrested Mama at four o'clock Christmas morning. She was in her robe, so they ordered her to dress at once. She was to accompany them to Headquarters, though they did not say why.

Mama thought that she would return shortly. She was tossed into an unheated basement cell. Day after day she remained in isolation. There was no light except when a hole in the door was opened for food to be shoved through. The flagstone floor had a hole in one end for sanitation. A Nazi guard marched endlessly back and forth outside her cell. Mama later wrote about him:

> The cold ruthless expression of hate in his blue eyes—eyes like
> a snake's, devoid of any expression but evil, and the inhuman

twisted mouth with its sardonic grin. Bloodlust and cruelty were written all over his young blonde Aryan face.

Malnourished, exposed to cold, feverish, she was transported in the dark and dumped onto the ground, where she was left to die of "natural causes." Someone flashed a light on her face and commented, "Just another corpse." Struggling, she forced herself to stir. When it was seen that she was conscious, she was taken to a new holding area which she later discovered to be the Belsen concentration camp.

For the first three weeks, she was given apple juice accompanied by castor oil. When her weight fell below sixty-five pounds, she was given a variety of inadequate diets, a sadistic nurse working to keep her alert enough to realize that she was slowly dying. Mama later wrote:

> The dead and dying lay all about me. Some were not carried out for days, and I used to watch them being thrown into community graves, piled one on top of the other. The Brown Nurses, Nazi nurses in brown uniform, took especial delight in abusing and mistreating me. One, Schwester Elfrieda, had a grudge against all Americans, and me in particular, so took advantage of every opportunity of venting her spite on me. Every morning at four o'clock she would rip the coverings from me, and empty a pail of cold water over my fevered body. Then, raising me by the hair, she would slap my face and pinch my breasts till I fell limp in her arms.
>
> Although only twenty-three years of age, this nurse was a powerfully built woman who looked all of forty. Her great overdeveloped muscles were covered with layers of fat, and she had small vicious eyes like a pig's. She was a fanatical Nazi, with a venomous hate for everyone non-Aryan, and she worshiped Hitler as a god. Another of her special torments was taking supposed blood tests from me. Two or three times a day and often at night, she would come with her needle to pierce my arm at the elbow and relieve me of a phial of blood. The needle was dull and blunt, and in time my arm became badly infected. She also took perverse pleasure in collecting cockroaches and

39

beetles to put in my soup, or overturn a cupful of them into my bed. Or she would upset a pail of slops [urine and excrement] over me, and stand shaking with laughter, all her layers of fat rolling with the effort, as she watched my distress.

Later Mama learned that her slow "natural" death had been ordered by Josef Kramer. His viciousness was his downfall. After the war, she helped the Allies track him down and bring him to trial. He was executed.

While Mama was in Belsen, we four children were told that she was dead. Nine-year-old Joe was sent to the Hitler Youth Camp in Meissen, near Dresden. Philip was placed with a Nazi woman, and Valerie with a Nazi family. I was sent to Belsen, to live in the group home of a special elite SS school for training future leaders. I did not know that Mama was alive in a separate Belsen area. Whether in the death camp or the SS school, all the children remained hungry all the time. It was only a matter of degree.

We were forced to endure some of the tortures of those who were eventually murdered. Our punishment was to be a learning experience. The children who were abused in the death camps were being mistreated for the pleasure of the guards. The children who were abused in the SS–run homes were being taught discipline that was meant to strengthen us. We were to become tough, obedient, and instantly responsive to anything we were told to do. Along the way, we went through hell. My body was covered with welts and scars from the punishment.

One time I tried to run away from the camp. Naturally I was caught. To teach me discipline and obedience, I was placed in a bathtub filled with cold water, my wrists tied to the faucets, and forced to stay there all night.

Approximately four months after her arrest, Mama was released. She was dangerously ill, underweight, and at risk of dying. She managed to learn where I was living and demanded my release. When we saw one another, the emotions were overwhelming. I wept uncontrollably. Clinging to her, I knew that everything I had been told was a lie.

Our house had been partially destroyed by an incendiary bomb. The smell of phosphorous was still in the air. Mama's face was blue, bruised, distorted with pain. All her strength had been used in getting me and bringing me home. She collapsed on the bed in her room. She coughed and weakly whispered for water.

I brought Mama water to drink. I carried it in a cup, then fed it to her a spoonful at a time. I lay beside her. I tried not to sleep. I was terrified she would die. I was certain she would live only if I stayed awake.

One morning Mama awakened, hugged me, and smiled. The coughing had subsided and, though weak, she was able to get out of bed.

Not long after that, a drunk displaced person, Polish or Slavic, broke into the house. I hid behind the stairs of the basement, terrified, clutching a doll Mama had made for me. Mama was cautious with the man, going along in the way she handled him. She gave him a bottle of wine to satisfy his demands for more whiskey. The man swallowed it rapidly. It was filled with floor varnish. Before he knew what was happening to him, he dropped dead. We dragged him out to the field behind our house where bomb craters made natural graves. The night was black, and no one could see us as we placed him in a crater and covered him with dirt and snow. Mama had saved us from danger once again, and death.

The war intensified around us. Our back yard and street front became camouflaged tank traps. I could see German machine gunners on every corner. Bremen aflame . . . the sky crackling in orange-red leaping flames . . . glow of hot cinders . . . a lasting memory.

MARITA

The Russian army was the first to crash through the lines of the German defenders in our city. Eventually a U.S. Army Jeep pulled up in front of our home. American soldiers helped Mama retrieve my brothers and sister, and with British forces, located me in Belsen. She became an interpreter and translator for them, working in headquarters doing intelligence. We learned that Papa was alive. He had been passing intelligence to the Allies and was released unharmed from the camp in England. Mother began making plans for us to live in the United States.

The nightmare that followed began as a birthday party. I was seven. My sister and I were friends with the daughter of an American sergeant who lived down the street from us. My mother was delighted because she wanted us to feel comfortable with Americans.

No one realized that the sergeant was an extremely sick and dangerous man. He had risen to a position of leadership during the war, when it was possible for a psychopath to take actions that are seemingly heroic.

During my friend's party, her father lured all of us children into the basement of his house to play a game of Blind Man's Bluff. The basement was dark, and we were all told to hide. I heard the sergeant fumble with my sister. She broke loose and raced up the stairs. I tried to follow my sister, but I was suddenly grabbed and thrown onto a pad. I heard the other children running upstairs.

The man's hand covered my mouth and nose. He kneeled on my body, pinning me down as he tore at my clothes and undid his pants. He warned me not to say anything, that he would kill me if I told. I remember fighting for air, and the searing pain as he penetrated my body. Then I blacked out.

I awakened in agony. Slowly, painfully I made my way up the stairs. I went outside, crawling when my legs failed to support me, leaving a trail of blood as I made my way home.

THE FIRST ASSASSINATION

Mama was near hysteria. She took me to the 69th Station U.S. military hospital where I was examined and kept for observation.

The sergeant was arrested. I was taken home. Mama stayed with me constantly, hugging me, cuddling me. She told me I would get well, that my life would return to normal. She said I had to face up to him, to put him away.

I was taken to the Navy compound in Bremerhaven. A court martial was being held. The U.S. military prosecutor said, "Point to the man who made you hurt." I sensed him to the left of me, said his name, then turned and pointed at him.

He was sentenced to ninety-nine years in prison, no parole. I later learned that he had been molesting his daughter, and that he had raped and murdered one other little German girl.

9

The CIA noted my record as a victim of violence. Their plan was a vicious one. Its purpose was to disinform, to turn Castro into a villain who deserved to be killed.

When I arrived in New York from Havana in 1959, I was anemic, suffering from septicemia, and in need of a D and C to stop my bleeding. The day after I arrived, I was taken to Roosevelt Hospital for the D and C.

At the hospital, several FBI agents, supplemented by detectives from the New York Police Department, acted as guards and interrogators. Alexander I. Rorke put a large cross at the head of my bed. A suicide watch was posted in case of postnatal depression.

My X-rays and medical records were shared with the FBI and CIA. They proved there had been a live birth, not an abortion. I was told that the baby, seven and a half months along, was born alive, and was now dead. The agents later showed me two glossy four-by-five colored photos of what appeared to be a bloody infant boy's corpse, mutilated and dismembered, on a bedspread exactly like the one in Fidel's and my room in the Havana Hilton.

The security was not so tight that it kept a determined person from my room. One of Fidel's aides, Pedro, bribed a guard at a moment when only one was there, and slipped in to see me. Pedro told me that my baby was alive and well, and that Fidel loved me and wanted me to return. He also brought a document for me to sign that stated that Fidel had nothing to do with the horrors I had experienced. I knew it was true and tried to sign it, but I was too weak and managed to get only my first name. As I struggled to finish, the guards discovered Pedro, who silently slipped away.

The CIA was experimenting with mind control techniques. In the weeks and months ahead, I was exposed to some of them. The idea, similar to that of the Belsen SS camp, was to limit my access to information and to other people, to reward actions and attitudes that fit what the group wanted, and to avoid or belittle anything that differed. I was to be isolated especially from people who might influence me or present information other than what the FBI wanted me to know.

I was quiet, sullen, withdrawn. I missed Fidel. I missed my life in Havana. I felt trapped and wanted to scream against the constant supervision.

Gradually, the agents made themselves my friends and started to draw me into their world. They used "love-bombing," a technique similar to that of religious cult groups in recruiting new members. In my loneliness and isolation, they became like a family to me.

There were two FBI agents named Frank—Frank O and Frank L, both kind and decent individuals. They were close associates of Alexander Rorke, a gentle, loving eloquent man who worked for the FBI and was involved with covert operations sponsored by the CIA. I became very fond of Alex. His compassion and sorrow for me were genuine. He was convinced of the truth of his thinking and sincerely wanted to help me. As our closeness developed, I came to call him my "big brother."

Alex was a deeply religious Catholic. As a young man, he had gone to seminary at Loyola University to become a Jesuit priest. For him, the fight against Castro and any other Communist who threatened the moral and political fabric of our nation was a holy war. "Communism," he repeatedly explained to me, "is an ungodly evil." In his mind, Castro was the Antichrist and Armageddon was in Havana.

I had no formal religious training growing up. I associated religion with the wonders of nature. Alex was concerned about my eternal soul. He took me to a Catholic church to pray. He talked about religion all the time, trying to convert me. He told me that killing was wrong, but sometimes God wants us to kill someone bad for Him. It would be alright with God if I killed Fidel, for example, even though it would be sinful for me to hurt someone else. I had been sinning when I was impregnated by Fidel, while unmarried. Fidel and his associates had sinned when they killed my baby. However, if I eliminated Fidel, I could make myself right with God. Alex was the second person to suggest that I eliminate Fidel.

From the time I left the hospital, Alex and the other CIA agents kept repeating that Castro was behind the "murder" of my baby. "The Communist Butcher Castro," they called him. They showed me a note from a doctor which said that, because of the way I had been treated, I could never have another child.

They said Fidel had to destroy me because I was bad for the revolution. I was of German birth and an American citizen. The Cuban people who supported Fidel would never stand for such a woman to be so intimately involved in his life. They would never allow me to take a prominent role in postrevolution Cuba. It was only by chance that I was alive at all.

No one discussed Pedro, the Cuban man who had come to see me in the hospital. I did not feel it was safe to mention anything that might contradict them.

My mother had flown home from her assignment in Europe to be with me, and was under orders to help them use me for propaganda, to destroy the image of Castro as a revolutionary hero, to make him into a monster and build support against him. An article conceived by agents and bylined by her was to be published by *Confidential* magazine. This magazine specialized in exposing the disreputable actions and lives of organized criminals, Hollywood stars, and politicians. For example, *Confidential* broke the stories of Rock Hudson and Liberace being homosexual. An estimated twelve million people read each issue. It was as sleazy as it was popular, the perfect place for an "exclusive" American intelligence "leak" about Castro.

The cover page set the tone for the article: AN AMERICAN MOTHER'S TERRIFYING STORY—"FIDEL CASTRO RAPED MY TEENAGE DAUGHTER." The subtitle was: LURED TO CUBA BY CASTRO, MARITA LORENZ, 18, WAS KIDNAPPED, RAPED AND THEN CRUELLY ABORTED!

The story accused Castro of a list of ten crimes, including false promises, kidnapping, rape, isolation, drugging, intimidation, violation of rights, forced abortion, and continuing harassment.

The article made clear that my mother was a U.S. government employee and had been for thirteen years, and that she was a cousin of Henry Cabot Lodge, U.S. Ambassador to the United Nations.

The seduction, as described by the article, was chaste and verbal. Castro seduced my mind, verbally convincing me to go to Cuba as his personal guest, providing me with a diplomatic ticket from the Cuban Consulate. However, once there, I was supposedly kept locked in a room in the Havana Hilton and guarded by rifle-toting soldiers for four days before Fidel lowered himself to see me.

The rape scene was melodramatic, meant to arouse the anger of Americans against Fidel. Supposedly we talked for a half hour before he removed his jacket and shirt, and insisted I take off my clothes. Against my protests and pleading, my struggling and weeping, he tore off my clothes. I showed him the cross on my necklace chain, and he furiously tore it off. The he brutally ravaged me.

The melodrama continued. The article said that, between the violence of the rape and Fidel's weight, I had a slipped disc in my spine so painful that I could not walk for three days. I pleaded for a doctor, but Fidel didn't want anyone to know how terrible he had been to me. Even when I began to recover, according to the article, I was regularly drugged so that he could return and have his way with me as often as he liked.

The article told of my talking about religion with Fidel, though such discussions always fell on deaf ears. He was a dictator who had turned his back on God, a murderer who threatened to force me to watch the executions regularly taking place just outside the hotel. However, the one saving grace was that he offered to marry me. I accepted because, as a good girl, marriage would at least help me "erase the shame" in my heart.

The story continued with Castro supposedly keeping me hidden from the people he feared most—the American press. Then, after our return from New York, Fidel made every effort to have me lose the baby.

Captain Jesús Yanez Pelletier, the article maintained, informed me at pistol point that I would never leave Cuba alive with Castro's baby in my belly. When drugs failed to cause me to miscarry, he beat and pounced on my stomach.

THE FIRST ASSASSINATION

Ultimately I escaped, as in real life. But I paid for my sins. My five and a half month old fetus was cruelly murdered, and I was sterile.

The story sounds almost humorous when read today. It is like watching a very bad B-movie. In those days, the Cold War encouraged a style of writing that placed America and Americans in positions of heroism, defending women in Hell.

When I look back today, it seems odd that I didn't rebel, that I didn't explode with anger and rail against what was happening. But the enclosed world in which I was being nursed back to health was designed to suck me into a bad dream where these red-blooded, God-fearing, all-American heroes had rescued me, a half-dead, traumatized girl sent back from Cuba, from the clutches of Fidel Castro, Antichrist and butcher. I withdrew into silence.

The agents overseeing me made certain I could not think clearly. Then they wore down any lingering resistance with "vitamin" tablets, the kind of vitamins that had become fashionable with the patients of Park Avenue doctors. The vitamins were laced with amphetamines at levels that were addictive. I was kept wired, my metabolism working overtime, my weight dropping, my sleep limited by the excess artificial energy.

I was constantly restless. I would sit down to write a letter to Fidel, then find I could not think clearly enough to do it. Instead I had to get up and clean the apartment, go for a walk, or engage in some similar activity. I needed to move, not reason.

My appetite was almost nonexistent. The agents would make certain I took my "vitamin" immediately upon awakening, washing it down with strong black coffee. They told me that the black coffee was part of the "therapy" to help me regain my health.

I normally need at least eight hours of sleep to function,

and have since I was a little girl. So long as I was taking the "vitamins," though, the earliest I went to bed was two o'clock in the morning, and frequently it would be after three o'clock before I slept. Then I would always get up at six A.M., having my coffee and "vitamin" as I was dressing.

Had I understood what was happening, I would have stopped when I saw how my body was reacting when I was late with the pills. I took so many at such consistent times that, if I delayed the pill for some reason, I would become overwhelmingly exhausted. It was as though my body was saving up all the tiredness I would normally have felt from far too little sleep, too little food, and general malnutrition, hitting me with the need to sleep until yet another pill masked the exhaustion.

Years later I was able to obtain documents proving that the government was experimenting with mind control, chemical manipulation of thoughts, and other ways to convince people to take actions previously against their moral codes. Since I suffered from the emotional devastation of having had my baby taken from my womb, then supposedly murdered, I was a prime candidate for experimentation. And since my health was bad, my diet terrible, and I was getting little sleep, it was easy to convince me to go along with whatever the people closest to me wanted. Those individuals were always either government agents or people eager to achieve the same ends as the government. I was dragged around New York like a banner being waved by anti-Castro forces looking for publicity.

I never ate breakfast. Lunch was always junk food, such as a hamburger or cheeseburger provided by the agents. Dinner was at a coffee shop. I was still "flying" from the amphetamine "vitamins," so never wanted a balanced meal. My complexion grew pale, sallow, yet I could not stop.

I had a strong interest in the news when I returned to the United States, but the agents did not let me read the newspapers or news magazines, nor did they let me listen to the news on the radio. They told me it was not interesting. They told me I needed to read what they provided, all of which was either anticommunist or anti-Castro literature. Trying to be a dutiful daughter, I read what I could until concentrating became so difficult, the writing made no sense.

Always I was applauded for my "courage," pitied for what I had "endured," and encouraged to hate Fidel. Over and over again I was told that Fidel had killed my baby.

To further the propaganda, my mother had to file a lawsuit against the Cuban government for $11 million. The sum was chosen to be certain the story was carried in the press. Fidel was sent a bill for my operation in Roosevelt Hospital. The government planned to use the paid receipt as "proof" that he had taken my baby.

Eventually I received a telegram from Fidel, asking me to call him. He included the telephone number I knew was his private line. I hurried over to a pay telephone on Riverside Drive, still accompanied by my bodyguards from the FBI, so the agents, though able to listen to my side could not record the conversation on what I suspected was a tapped telephone at home.

The agents stood so close that they were able to hear Castro tell me that the baby was fine, that the aide would be jailed for what he had done to me if he could be found (he had fled the island or gone into hiding), and that the doctor had been shot. He wanted me to come back to Cuba, and he wanted to talk with my father.

When Fidel said that the baby was beautiful, that he was in a nursery, the agents panicked. They grabbed the receiver and hung it up.

In December 1959, I received another telegram to call Fidel. I decided to sneak outside, going to the same telephone booth on Riverside Drive that I used whenever I wanted privacy. I never thought that my consistency would cause the FBI to tap that line and keep the phone booth under surveillance.

It was late at night when I went to use the telephone. I was under active surveillance by the FBI, with at least two men always so close at hand; I could do nothing without their knowledge. The phone booth was located near a park, very much in the open. As I dialed the operator to begin placing the call, I closed the door so I could hear better. Just as I did, one of the panes of glass shattered. I was unhurt, though terribly embarrassed. I thought I had closed the door with too much force.

Then there was a whistling sound, and a bullet penetrated the frame near my head. I ducked down as a third shot struck at a point that would have killed me had I not moved. A sniper had honed in on me and was trying to kill me.

Dropping low, I raced from the phone booth. I reached the Soldiers' and Sailors' Monument in Riverside Park, moving around it and using it for cover. I heard footsteps pursuing me, waited until they were coming from a direction that kept the monument between us, and then ran again.

I reached West End Avenue, then Broadway. Finally I returned to West Eighty-seventh Street and my parents' apartment. I had eluded the sniper, though the agents were still nowhere in sight. It was only a half hour later that my "protectors," carrying their lunch, showed up. They were allowed a break, but they had never taken it together before.

What did it mean? I have no idea. I may have been attacked by a pro-Batista Cuban. I may have been attacked by a government agent. With the *Confidential* magazine piece set for publication, my death would have added to the hate against Castro. Fidel could have been accused of ordering my death since his men had failed to kill me in Havana. I was important only as propaganda.

After working in intelligence off and on for most of my adult life, and after talking with my mother about her work as a high up official with NSA, I now believe rogue agents of the government tried to silence me. The uncharacteristic action of the agents assigned to guard me, the extreme hatred for Fidel, and the excesses of those fighting the Cold War all make me feel I had been set up. My mother knew nothing of this, though she would have been even easier to use against America's enemies had she believed I was killed on orders from Fidel. The times were very different from today. The idea of killing someone the government saw as an immoral, out-of-control teenager for the "good" of the nation was acceptable covert action.

10

In late December, just before the article came out, the CIA sent me on a dry run to Cuba to test how Fidel would react to me. I was half crazy with worry and anger when I reached the Havana Hilton. I wanted to see my baby, but Fidel would not allow it. He said he did not know exactly where the baby was being kept.

Again Fidel made it clear that I could have my baby only if I returned to Cuba for good, to be with him, with our son, with the Cuban people. The three of us could be a family, but I was neither going to remove our son from Cuba nor was I going to expose him to the risks inherent in his allowing a brief visit. In Cuba, a child born to a Cuban father belongs to the father.

Camilo Cienfuegos was missing. In late October, two weeks after I left Cuba, he disappeared while flying to see Fidel. Years later, a CIA operative offered a deathbed confession to me: he admitted Camilo, who had shown such loving kindness to me, who had saved my life at the Havana Hilton, had been killed by the CIA with C-4 plastics used to down his helicopter.

My meeting with Fidel was a bit tense—so much had

happened. At the same time, it was as if nothing had happened. We still seemed to be where we both belonged when we were together. My situation was complex. For me to stay in Cuba, as he suggested, would mean unbearable pressure from the FBI, the CIA, and the anti-Castro Cubans the government wanted me to work with.

After two days, I returned to New York. I was numb and silent. To build up my distrust of Fidel, the government agents showed me, as they had repeatedly before, the pictures of my dismembered baby and the doctor's note saying I was sterile from the forced delivery.

Just before the *Confidential* article came out, my parents, the FBI, and the N.Y.P.D. decided that I should return to Germany with my father. The idea was to protect me from the repercussions of people in New York recognizing me. I also wanted the solitude and quiet.

In Germany my sanctuary and peace were shattered when I passed a newsstand and saw a picture of me and Fidel on the front page of the German magazine *Stern*. It was a version of the *Confidential* article. In Germany, as in America, I had become a public figure.

I took my father's Mercedes and drove to Denmark, Belgium, Holland. Everywhere I went, headlines followed me. I shunned people, disguised myself, used my accents. I was recognized at each border crossing. I stuck to country roads.

In Holland I enjoyed myself driving along dikes and walking in the midst of a magnificent sea of tulips. I shall never forget the beauty and tranquility. On my left, all the way to the horizon, there were yellow tulips; on the right, red tulips spread under a cloudless blue sky. An old man on a donkey cart greeted me. He didn't know or care who or what I was in the public world, far away.

In the darker days to come, I would block out violent, ugly situations by thinking back to that sea of tulips.

11

The fall of 1959 was a period of great tension, both in the United States and abroad. Communism was perceived to be on the march. When Nikita Kruschev began denouncing the west, he talked of "burying" America.

Large city police departments were quietly establishing units to investigate "subversives," but privately they called themselves the "red squads." Anyone seeking change in the existing social order was considered a "Commie," a "pinko," or a "fellow traveler."

Fidel Castro was depicted as the most evil leader in the western hemisphere. Certainly there were right-wing dictators in South and Central America who were denying their citizens freedom. Such men were using assassination, torture, and media control to keep their subjects living in terrified submission. But they were "good" bad guys, men who would not tolerate Communist totalitarianism. The danger came from Fidel.

Cuba was a small island with fewer inhabitants than New York City. The country was in economic turmoil, and while he would eventually involve his people in a variety of guerrilla wars, especially in Angola, that was not even a consideration at the time. His position was as yet too unstable to be able to control his own country effectively, muchless export revolution. And as President Eisenhower well knew, Castro wanted to be accepted by the United States government in the early days following the overthrow of Batista.

The CIA had many operatives in Cuba during this period. Their intelligence confirmed the truth of everything I was saying. Yet in the minds of the rabid anticommunists, Fidel was the Antichrist.

Day after day the true menace of my former lover was explained to me. Only the most paranoid believed he would make a military move against Miami, though a number of residents did arm themselves in case of that eventuality. The real plan was to move west, then north through Mexico, spreading his revolutionary tentacles. Some of the agents and anti-Castro Cubans told me of plans he harbored for moving through Honduras, Guatemala, and Bélize (then British Honduras). From there he would reach Mexico, capturing and, I suppose, raping the bikini-clad, capitalistic female tourists in Acapulco. Then it would be north through Mexico City, perhaps Chihuahua, Ciudad Juarez, and Tijuana. He would have his men take Arizona, Texas, Los Angeles. The Cubans would subvert the minds and hearts of the young, spreading like uncontrollable cancer cells, destroying a great nation that had previously been the shining light of democracy.

Everything I was given to read, everyone with whom I was encouraged to talk, made it clear that Fidel Castro represented the greatest danger the U.S. had faced since Pearl Harbor, and that only through his elimination would western civilization survive.

I wanted to have a serious talk about what was being said

with my parents, but that was impossible. My father was at sea. My mother would be home one day, and the next day her bags would be packed and she would be on her way to another city, another country. Her security clearance was so high, her work so classified, that she could not tell me where she would be. I could reach her only through a post office box where her mail was carefully forwarded. She called only from safe phones whose origin could not be traced.

The pressure on me grew more intense when the Marines began talking about the possibility of their base on Guantanamo being attacked by Castro. I was told that intelligence reports revealed that Fidel was going to kill every American on the naval base. Then, with the notoriety such violence would create, he would intimidate, infiltrate, and conquer his Latin neighbors as he began his insidious, seemingly invincible march north.

I tried to argue at times. I had just returned from being with him. Surely I would have seen activity that indicated his troops were massing for conquest and there was none. There were uniformed supporters throughout Havana, but then this was not an organized army. They did little more than act as a national police force.

No one wanted to hear my reasoning. They had "inside information" gathered by professional spies (one overdramatic, exaggerating asshole operative) who knew far more about Castro's Cuba than I did. I had to trust them.

The stories grew worse. There were tales of Americans held captive and tortured under orders by Castro. I had not witnessed or heard about anything like that. Yet I half-believed the agents when they told me such stories. As tired and overwhelmed as I was, it made sense when they explained that Fidel made certain I saw none of the horrors. I was a tool of Communist propaganda for him. He dared only let me see the best the revolution had to offer.

Vengeance was most frequently suggested as the reason I should take a life. Fidel killed my baby, I was told. Killing Fidel would avenge that death and save the United States from infiltration and destruction by Communist Cuban guerrillas.

The enthusiasm for the idea was intense. I met with FBI agents, CIA agents, and leaders in the Cuban anti-Castro movement living in and working from the United States. We met at the 69th Street office of the FBI, in restaurants, and in safe houses, especially Frank Nelson's apartment.

Always they would react first with sympathy for the loss of my baby. Then they would talk about how perfect I was, how I was the only person who could get close enough to Fidel to kill him. I was still in good standing with Fidel, they reminded me. I had the Lieutenant's uniform, and such uniforms continue to be worn by the insiders. I could move about anywhere without trouble. I also had the key to the rooms we shared, a key that was in the pocket of my uniform when I was flown out of the country. I was the perfect weapon.

It was an odd situation to be in. There were two groups of Cubans engaging in secret wars against each other, one supporting Castro, the other against him. I was made a member of both.

I was sent to meet with the pro-Fidel groups such as the 26th of July Movement at the La Barraca (The Barracks) restaurant in Manhattan. It was there that Fidel had told me to talk with two of his close friends. The two women loved Fidel and embraced me warmly. They knew I was a "Mama," knew I was Fidel's common-law wife.

At the same time, the agents had me join the anti-Castro White Rose Society and another group, the 2506 Brigade. Both wanted vengeance because they had been Batista supporters pushed out of power by the revolution. The White Rose Society was involved with planning Fidel's assassination, as well as other acts of violence. They were preparing to bomb Cuba's oil refineries and burn the sugar cane crops that provided most of the country's income. They also planned to kill Fidel's agents in the United States, which New Jersey based Omega 7 later did. Some members of the White Rose Society and the 2506 Brigade (later called Alpha 66, then Omega 7) were so dedicated that thirty years later they are still obsessed with Cuba. They continue to train paramilitary armies in South Florida for the assassination of Fidel Castro.

The entire situation was overblown and ridiculous. One day I would be in La Barraca, enjoying the people, talking about the Havana I loved. Then I would return home and encounter the agents who insisted I go to a White Rose meeting where I was expected to verbally attack Fidel, my "tormento." I was being both cultivated by the feds and followed because I was meeting with Fidel's intelligence agents in New York.

During this time I also met top American business executives whose companies had Cuban holdings under Batista. These were politically influential Americans seeking to recover their investments. They were delighted that I was going to be an assassin.

Soon I was told that I should go to Miami with the Brigade. I had tried to telephone Fidel, who was refusing to take my calls since the magazine article had come out. I wrote to him, but to no avail. There seemed nothing left for me except to travel to Miami with the CIA payrolled pros who kept telling me they were my friends. From there, with more indoctrination and instruction in how to kill, arrangements would be made for me to go ahead.

Fidel's death would not be unpleasant, I was assured. I would be given pills to slip into any liquid he was drinking. The pills would be odorless and tasteless, and the target would just slip off to sleep. The agents tried to paint an image in my mind of this specially concocted poison that would render him blissfully unconscious before it permanently stopped all bodily functions. I would not need to watch, to wait around to check on him. It was as though he would be sleeping like a baby as I left the room, so my last memory of him would be of my lover at peace, unable to scream. The poison paralyzed the vocal cords instantly.

I would have backup if there were any problems. The CIA maintained agents in Cuba who would spot check me. Americans were still moving freely about Havana, especially if they had been down there before the Castro takeover and were not known to be corrupt. No one knew who was legitimately there and who might be an intelligence agent.

I was to depart for Havana via Miami. I would be working for the CIA, which I was told was an honor for any American because they had the highest standards for intelligence operatives and covert activity. And I would be supported by important people from Chicago, apparently a sort of CIA auxiliary. Actually the Chicago people were Mafia.

The contract on Castro was arranged before John Kennedy took office, according to Mafioso Chuck Giancana, Sam's brother. Certainly other anti-Castro organizations were working with the FBI and others under the jurisdiction of President Eisenhower and Vice President Nixon from the beginning.

Allegedly there were to be three hits handled by the mob for the CIA. One was against Fidel, ultimately my assignment. The second was against Patrice Lumumba of the Congo who was killed in 1961 as part of the U.S. Government's covert operations in the Belgian Congo. The third was to be against Rafael Leonidas Trujillo Molina, a Dominican Republic leader who was also murdered that year.

Johnny Roselli was the first mobster to be approached about killing Castro. He then recruited Sam Giancana, who had been able to get his money out of Havana after the revolution, something Trafficante, Marcello, Lansky, and others had not. He ignored what he later claimed to his brother was a $150,000 fee offered for the hit. He knew that the CIA would be indebted to him if he took the contract because the casinos would be reopened after Castro was dead. The CIA had been getting a cut from the skimmings during the Batista years, and Giancana liked the idea of having the intelligence community in his debt. He agreed to be a party to the setup.

By the time I was talking with the Mafia leaders involved, the numbers had risen to a total of six million dollars, with one third payment made the moment Castro was dead. I would be a rich woman on the ground floor of a new career—America's premier female assassin.

Americans like their assassins to be a variation of Ian Fleming's character James Bond, Agent 007. If male, they should be well-educated gentlemen, sophisticated, dedicated to the laws of the nation, willing to risk their lives for God and country. Such agents should be at home in an exclusive gentleman's club, modest drinkers with discerning palates, and knowledgeable about art, music, and the latest literature. They should be masters of martial arts and weapons of violence, yet only consider using such skills for the few minutes every year or two when it is necessary to save the world from one new international madman or another.

Female assassins are conservatively dressed in expensively tailored outfits whose hemlines are never higher than an inch or two below the knees. They wear conservative hats, a single strand of cultured pearls, modest earrings, and white gloves whenever going into town. Their demeanor is a cross between that of the president of the Junior League and a parochial school nun who has a black belt in knuckle rapping. Such women are socially correct, flawlessly mannered "perfect ladies", yet capable of steely rigidity when dealing with waiters, maids, gardeners, bellmen, enemy agents, megalomaniacal Commie dictators bent on world conquest, and other inferiors.

Such people are community assets, the perfect couples to have next door, for neither their pets nor their children will ever misbehave. They can be counted upon to contribute to local charities, attend parent/teacher conferences, and keep their grass mowed in summer, their sidewalks shoveled in winter. Their profession may be a bit unusual, but they never bring home unpleasant "shop talk," decomposing corpses, or the smell of cordite and gunpowder. The fact that they sometimes kill people for a living goes unmentioned in the same manner that a janitor does not discuss the toilets he cleans, and an amusement park manager does not mention the vomit he has removed after a child insists upon overindulging in sweets, chili dogs, and soda pop before riding the roller coaster.

That is the American fantasy of an assassin. The truth in 1960 was quite different. I, for example, wore jeans and a sweet frilly blouse, sneakers or boots. No way did I look like Mata Hari.

In fact, had John Kennedy learned what was taking place in the Florida training camps of CIA contract agents and Cuban exile counterrevolutionaries, he might not have died. He might have either handled the men in the camps differently or recognized the danger they represented to anyone they perceived as not being totally on their side. Instead, he read the novels of Ian Fleming, idealized the image of James Bond, and was murdered by real agents whose loyalty was to a fantasy of power and vengeance. Some renegade counterrevolutionaries were trained with the aid of an organization whose officials truly believed their psychopathic whims could be acted upon without the constraints of the American Constitution they supposedly were sworn to uphold.

The training CIA contract employees, mercenaries, and Washington supported Cuban counterrevolutionaries were receiving was totally opposite the "Christian ethic" right-wingers claim is the basis for America. First there is the attitude towards murder. It is considered not ethical to take a life other than in wartime when violence is required to conquer or defend territory. I was indoctrinated into a world where life was expendable, where learning to kill is as standard a rite of passage as a teenager's learning to drive an automobile. It is just another tool for doing a job, though in the case of the CIA, that job may be to cause political change or domestic upheaval by murdering a legitimate leader.

The FBI was well aware of a CIA established camp in the Florida Everglades where the alligators might find protection, but human morality was an endangered species. Mercenaries, CIA contract agents, and anti-Castro forces gathered there to master scuba diving, to kill with knives, guns, garrotes, and bare hands, to poison and maim, to steal, to bomb, to sabotage, and to commit arson. The area was isolated enough so that no outsiders could see the ruthlessness of the training the participants received. And when tempers flared into violence, or a suspected counterspy was eliminated, no one could hear the screams. Silence is for sale in Miami in general, especially among hot-shot lawyers.

The idea was to limit the movement of this batch of carefully trained patriots and psychopaths to the training area when they were not on a mission wreaking covert havoc outside the country. But leaving them in Florida and expecting them to limit their activities to the Everglades training camp and mainland Cuba was like removing the bars from a zoo and operating on the honor system. Lions, tigers, and bears would have to give their word that they would not hunt and eat their natural prey to which they suddenly had easy access.

So went confinement in the Everglades. The troops, true carnivores, needed to roam. Their natural environment fell outside the conventions of polite society. Wherever they went, armories were stripped of weapons; private yachts were stolen, used for gun running, then destroyed; and innocent people died. I know. I was one of their conscripts.

Frank Nelson was a sometimes agent who enjoyed the business of death, particularly the pay. He liked to own weapons used in kills. He enjoyed selling weapons to people who killed. And he was fortunate enough to associate with and profit from the two organizations eager to indulge in his lifelong labor of love—the Central Intelligence Agency and the Mafia families that dominated American organized crime. Nelson was the CIA's associate money man and organizer on the East Coast. Fronting as a salesman he was also a conduit for Mafia-executed operations endorsed by the covert action leaders of the CIA. His large Manhattan apartment overlooking Central Park was a safe haven, a place where meetings could be held, explosives stored, and everyone could speak freely—as long as you had been screened first by a phone call and passed the body frisk on arrival.

I entered Nelson's world because he worked with the agents assigned to me after my return from Cuba in 1959. He was helping to coordinate the assassinations of Fidel, and I was taken to his apartment to formally meet the man who would become a major factor in my life. This was Frank Fiorini, a former Marine, CIA contract agent, and mercenary whose loyalties seemed to rest with whomever paid the most for his services. He was in the mountains in Cuba with supplies for Fidel. He supplied anti-Castro forces as well. He was at the

Havana Riviera when Raúl, Camilo, and I were examining the gambling casino facilities. And he was in Florida, training anti-Castro defectors—and anyone else who wanted to join in the wargame. He is still hard at work today.

The name Fiorini never became widely known. Perhaps he did not want to be reminded of his Italian ancestry, or perhaps he thought that people might connect him with the Mafia. Whatever the case, he used the name Frank Sturgis, the name now found in most books on the history of the 1960s. If covert action was necessary, whether the Bay of Pigs, the assassination of a foreign leader, destabilization of a government or the Watergate break-in for the Nixon Committee to Reelect the President, Sturgis was there, was on his way, or had been apprehended en route.

Frank Fiorini/Sturgis towered almost a foot over me as he rose to greet me in Frank Nelson's apartment. He remembered me from the Havana Riviera, and he knew I remembered him. He also knew what happened to me. He told me he was glad to welcome me back to the "good old U.S.A.—alive!" Then he smiled, the upturned movement of his mouth almost mechanical. His snake eyes looked hard and cold. Unlike a snake, they were constantly alert, seeing all, periodically lighting on one person or another, trying to read their souls with his gaze, then moving on. He was the perpetual predator, seeming to divide all living things into one of two categories—the weak, to be ignored (or crushed if they got in the way), and the quarry, to be taunted, trapped, and then eliminated. His clothing was nondescript, his speech unrefined. He did not drink or smoke. He lived only for the money, the glory, the thrill of violence. The fame he longed for never materialized. He was to live a soldier of misfortune.

I was told that "Sturgis" was a man who controlled the Southern part of Miami, with Eduardo, his paymaster. I never knew if this meant Florida or outside the United States. Eduardo rose to infamy as E. Howard Hunt, Watergate burglar.

Sturgis and I shook hands, and even the physical touch of the man was intimidating. The "welcome aboard" handshake felt more like a warning grasp, the unspoken message of which was, "You fuck up, you die." Later some of us who tried to leave the world of the CIA realized that the attitude of the leadership, both career and contract agents like Sturgis was, "The CIA is a 'choo-choo train.' You get on and go for the ride wherever it takes you, and along the way you do your job. If you fuck up or back out, the choo-choo will run you over."

Sturgis embodied the distorted world view about which the FBI agents had warned me. Men like Rorke had talked God and country, pride, integrity, guts, about a patriotism that occasionally required an American to take a life for a higher good. Sturgis, by contrast, was violence personified. He was the man who would carefully instruct me to destroy another human, to find the most vulnerable parts of the intended victim in order to crush a windpipe, render someone blind or mute, to use everyday objects to puncture the heart or the brain. Where others had worked on my mind, his job was to develop my body into a killing machine.

I absorbed everything. I was like a child playing a forbidden game. I was winning approval. Finally, I was rewarded with an appointment to the most prestigious, top secret unit, Operation 40. I was the only female covert operative of the time.

I was willing to yield to peer pressure. I stopped looking for a means of escape and started trying to reinforce my decision that what I was engaged in was in the best interest of national security. I knew I was committed as I stood there in Frank Nelson's apartment, talking with Frank Fiorini/Sturgis. And I lied to myself that Fidel would only be knocked out, incapacitated, but not killed. Having been sucked in, I went along.

I tried to prepare to do battle against Fidel. *He* had left me, I told myself. *He* had put impossible pressures on me. *He* had taken my son and kept him for himself.

I tried to hate him. I tried to rouse myself to such over-whelming anger that I could relish the thought of taking vengeance against him. And yet, the more I tried to despise him, the more I knew I was lying, and I hated myself for the position I was in. I wept bitterly, angrily hitting my pillow or a wall or a fellow agent until, exhausted, I fell into a troubled sleep.

Rather than risk my backing out, when my fellow agents staying in the next room heard my tears, my pacing, my anguish, they "helped" me to relax with sedatives strong enough to keep me groggy in the morning. Then, when they wanted me functional, they gave me coffee and a stimulant that made me energetic to the point of recklessness. Kill Fidel? Why not? I had nothing better to do that year. And yet, as I yielded to such thoughts, another part of me rebelled.

The preparations continued. I was given numerous tests to fill out. There were forms and questions. I was studied for stress, for mental instability, for anything that might cause me to deviate from the purpose for which I was intended.

I was given permission to call Fidel and some of the aides I knew in Cuba, telling them that I planned to return. Fidel did not respond personally, but I was able to leave word that I would be coming back to the island. Forewarned, he would have no suspicion, or so Strugis and the others believed. I still did not know if I would choose to stay there. I was living each day as it came. Calling ahead was my way of letting Fidel know I was still considering his desires.

Much of the time was spent collecting supplies I would need. The CIA, including the contract agents, has almost unlimited money from which to draw. Anything an operative wants for a job is available, including solo time to think things out. I was given an expensive Minox Camera, tourist clothes, and other supplies.

I settled into a routine. I didn't think. I didn't question. I just took orders.

Every trip from New York was meant to serve multiple purposes. The one to Miami was no different. Our cars were converted to store handguns, machine guns, explosives, shells. There were dismantled weapons in the trunk, on the floor, and even under my feet. Two operatives sat in the front, three in the back. It was a six-day drive.

We were traveling at night. I tried to sleep as much as possible. Sturgis was there, along with Manuel, a Cuban who was part of the CIA and an ardent spokesperson against Fidel, often decrying the rape and abuse endured by so innocent a girl. He was rather a fool, but he was a skilled communicator and fund raiser. My story told at gatherings of wealthy sympathizers invariably raised thousands of dollars for "the cause."

After we stopped at the CIA training camp at Camp Perry, Virginia, we were joined by more cars. We were instructed to "take back roads," keep low key, have no contact with locals or the police. We camped out en route—nineteen men and me—hot, dirty, tired.

In Miami we were housed in the Riverside Motel, a pleasant, sky-blue inexpensive facility that looked like hundreds of others in the area of Miami, No Name Key, and the Everglades, our various points of operation. The rooms were small but comfortable, ideal for an elderly couple or young family on a budget. In fact, it was a safe house, a place made secure against outside intruders, where individuals involved in counterrevolutionary training could live and relax. It was operated like any other motel, except tourists always discovered there were no vacancies. During quiet times, it was not unusual to see a guest sitting in the lobby, observing us disassembling, cleaning, and reassembling a handgun or rifle.

Everyone was serious. The emphasis was on working as a group, on physical conditioning, on basic skills such as marksmanship, martial arts, knife fighting, survival.

Everyone had a different motive for being there. For the most part we were not psychopaths, sociopaths, or serial killers. Perhaps that is what made us so dangerous. We knew what we were doing, knew we were violating the norms of conventional society, but no one opposed us. We were looked upon with awe by outsiders. We experienced what the gods of Mt. Olympus must have felt when they disguised themselves as mortals and walked about the land. They could do anything to anyone with impunity because they *were* gods, not mortals.

We understood the law. We understood right from wrong. Even the church went along, calling us "liberators" and "freedom fighters." Yet by the time training was complete, we understood that we were above all that, delighting in playing cat and mouse with the Washington officials who only thought they were running the American government. How many times gullible Washington was taken in!

I witnessed the deliberate dispatching of inaccurate intelligence reports to the CIA, various intelligence officials, the President, and his advisers. This was done for any number of reasons.

The anti-Castro counterrevolutionaries were men who hated Castro, who were loyal to Batista, and were willing to give up their lives in order to "free" their country. They needed guns, ammunition, boats, and other equipment they could not afford. They knew that the CIA covert action funds being channeled to them were unlimited, but would be stopped if Washington did not think that Fidel was an imminent danger to American security. It was in their best interests to exaggerate, even lie in reports of Castro's hold over the Cuban people, his popularity, the size of his army, the strength of that military, and his plans to export revolution. Sometimes the numbers were dramatically increased. Sometimes fake "secret plans" were passed along as though actually obtained through clandestine sources such as disgruntled employees in Fidel's government. Always the purpose was to assure a steady supply of money for the war of liberation they fantasized launching and winning.

Mercenaries and contract agents dispatched false intelligence to insure they would have a steady income. They committed crimes and occasionally murder without risk of retaliation. It was the best job they could imagine having and they didn't want to have anyone take it away from them.

They also played practical jokes and sent dispatches meant to get a shocked reaction from national leaders and Congress. Could they create a story that would put the Strategic Air Command on red alert? Could they get immense emergency funds allocated to us to stop an imaginary guerrilla force moving through—say, Mexico City? About the only thing they didn't try was telling the White House that the Miami Senior Citizens Center was a Communist-front group where blue-haired ladies retired from Brooklyn had poison-gas cartridges in their walkers and bald old men had golf carts equipped with antiaircraft missile launchers.

No one ever caused a war with their lies. Instead, they cost—and continue to cost—the United States hundreds of millions of dollars. Because we were so special, it did not matter. For us, it was "normal," routine. We were like children in the world's most expensive overnight camp, only ours was run by obsessed military men like Frank Fiorini/Sturgis, the camp counselor from Hell.

I did not realize that I was being trained for life. My fantasy was that I would have one mission, succeed or fail. My frustration, fear, and anger would supposedly be finite.

To an outsider, I must have made an odd looking spy in Wrangler jeans and boots. My body was toned to perfection from the physical training. I was conversant with several languages, and I was being taught the language of spies—cryptography, jargon, what might be called "spookspeak." I was a woman desired by men, of special importance to my country. And I was also a drugged girl who, between the sleeping pills and the stimulants, withdrew to play with a pet turtle, a pet cat, and a baby doll I had saved from childhood and snuck in with my clothing when I left New York. Each night, when all was quiet and I was left alone, I would take out the doll and the pets. I brought water in my canteen for the turtle, stashed cat food in my pack. It was a ritual that went back to my childhood. I have always loved animals and during the war days, persisted in rescuing strays and bringing them back home to care for them in the safety of our darkened basement.

Was I unstable? Not by the standards of the CIA. Not in the world of the Cuban counterrevolutionaries. Not by comparison with some of the men with whom I trained.

I remember one time when we were all camping overnight, one of the foreign recruits tried to masturbate himself. He took out his penis and began stroking. He was gentle with himself. He was forceful with his stroking. He did everything he could to make himself erect, and nothing happened. He was oblivious, not only to me but to everyone else, lost in his own world of self-seduction and manual eroticism, and the object of his affection had spurned his hand. Finally, still unable to satisfy himself, he grabbed his rifle and began firing wildly into the air. The barrel had become his erection and the bullets his ejaculation. It was an incident more terrifying than humorous, and everyone pretended they were unaware of what had taken place.

By contrast, the tough female assassin dressing her baby doll seemed almost rational. Yet to hear what was said in Congress, the Pentagon, and the CIA, we represented a major force of national security, were freedom fighters confronting the ills of Central America.

There were times I felt like two different people. I may have been in training to be a tough guy, but I never intended to forget I was a woman in full bloom. I looked forward to the cramps that accompanied my menstrual cycle each month as an excuse to bow out of some of the more physically demanding maneuvers. I didn't feel parachuting from a plane would enhance my skills as an assassin—although it was fun as hell. I was twenty years old, vital, passionate, and healthy. As a normal, all-American female, I reserved the right to wear hair curlers to target practice. Let the guys snicker, as long as I was a better marksman.

I was the only woman in their totally male world. I was being channeled for a special operations group, Operation 40. I trained to kill. I trained as I thought an assassin should train, with dedication. I learned about methods, devices, tactics, guns, explosives that at times scared the hell out of me. In that capacity I put all feminine, childlike, or girlish behavior behind me. I felt mean, nasty, tough. I never smiled or revealed any emotion in my face or in my body language. At target practice my bullseye was Fidel's face, placed there for me compliments of my gracious instructor, Frank Sturgis. I didn't complain, I took orders. I ate, slept, thought, and breathed death.

It was a way of blocking out the other me—my past, my scandal, my terribly aching heart, my love gone, possibly forever. They called me *Alemana Fria*, the Cold German,

73

especially just prior to my period when I became more naturally violent.

Guns were shipped to various drop points by water. In the early days, people donated vessels. Later we stole boats from the docks outside the homes of wealthy residents in the Miami area. We needed someone who understood navigation. From years at sea sailing with Papa, I knew about calculating weather, reading charts, fuel needs, tides, mileage, loading weight, and the other details of captaining a vessel.

I got to play pirate on a 36-foot Chris-Craft that had been gutted and converted to haul crates of U.S. automatic weapons. Taking her load points from No Name Key to a contact point in Central America, I kept a loaded .38 automatic in my back pants pocket at all times. The security of the pistol and the feeling of power and control at the wheel gave me a sense of freedom. Away from soldiering, I did not have to think about the murderous mission for which I was being trained. Alone at sea, I scanned the horizon, delighting in the space, the light, the solitude, the wonderous beauty of the Gulf, the sharks diving through the water, the flying fish leaping in and out of the waves. Sometimes, looking at the tranquil beauty, I just dumped the crates of weapons overboard, hoping to save even one poor soul from agony as a result of my merchant of death mission.

The sea was familiar. I had a radio, a compass/sextant, precise maps, depth and direction finders, food, fuel, various kits, other modern electronic equipment that go with captaining such a vessel. Papa used to fill my head with tales of King Neptune, ruler of the sea. As I traveled, I thought of Neptune, and of how Papa said that the sea was unpredictable, like a woman. A slight change in weather conditions could lead to sailors encountering cruel violence from the unmercifully cruel sea.

THE FIRST ASSASSINATION

Sometimes guilt, remorse, scepticism overcame me and I got angry at myself, not wishing to play war and not knowing how to get out of it. On those occasions I deliberately scuttled the vessel on which I was captain. I waited until I could blame it on weather conditions or overload, a way that no one would suspect. After all, none of the boats were meant for gun running. They were all selected for their size, then stripped and rigged for our needs. Those who made the rapid switch were not experts on sailing. They were carpenters and mechanics. They expressed their anger, as I pretended to do, by scorning the men who had handled the loading of the lost craft.

There were always more guns. There were always boats to steal. The CIA had unlimited money so far as we were concerned, and no one was going to investigate anything we did.

And so the days passed. I tried to avoid thinking about the reason I had been brought to Miami and the Everglades. After my childhood, I never wanted to see violence again, and yet here I was, wanting to prove to the men with whom I was training to kill that I was as strong and capable as they were. I loathed myself for letting myself be a pawn in a game from which I could walk off the board at any time I desired. Whose war was I fighting, I wondered, and did I do this to myself?

Trapped in the struggle, I withdrew into myself, becoming separate from the others. Instead of questioning me, the leaders became proud of my reaction. They called it the "dedicated mission kill syndrome." They were convinced that I was psyching myself up like an athlete before the big game, that I was internally preparing to murder Fidel. All their doubts about my ability seemed to end.

Alex Rorke talked privately with me about my struggles over my "mission." We debated the role of God in all this.

"Alex," I said, "God doesn't condone killing. This job isn't okay."

"Our hearts, souls, and minds belong to the government," he told me.

"We must get out and do good before it's too late," I told him. "Tell everybody to forget and not use my thing with Fidel."

Killing Fidel was the answer Alex insisted. I was going to end a "brutal dictatorship." We were not doing the deed for money, personal gain, or recognition. Those would be bad motivations. Our hearts were pure. Killing Fidel was right with God. "Don't make God mad," he said.

I leaned on him, trying to justify the unjustifiable.

12

The CIA agents in Havana had been trying to spot a routine in Fidel's activities. Fidel simply had no routine, no set pattern, which drove his enemies wild with frustration. It always made me laugh and say "I told you so."

They discovered that he was completely unpredictable except when he was going to make a speech on television. Then there was a schedule to meet, and he took advantage of his suite in the Havana Hilton. It was the suite for which I had the key. My arrival was to be synchronized with a speech. Cubana Airlines still flew to the island from Miami. I was to travel as a tourist. I had three days to get ready.

The plane was a small one, filled with Cuban and American tourists. A special pocket had been sewn into my slacks, the pills placed inside in such a way that they would not be found should I be searched. I carried a Leica camera, the most expensive German 35mm camera made and one of the best. Just what a wealthy tourist might own, it supported my image as one of the many Americans curious about Cuba. Besides, it was something I had always wanted, and when I told Sturgis that I needed it for my disguise, no one objected. There was no end to the money. I was given $6,000 in cash to carry in case I had trouble and needed to bribe the barbados or anyone—though I knew the barbados were legal and bribery futile. I also carried my old uniform into which I planned to change after arriving. As I embarked, Alex, my only family, my friend, smiled, squeezed my hand, reminded me, "For God and Country." I put my hands together as though praying.

The trip took thirty minutes. I went to the rest room during the flight, convinced that the pills might be discovered if my body was frisked. I decided to hide them somewhere else, somewhere they would not be found. The camera case was the logical answer, and a place I was also certain they would check. Likewise there were my boots, my socks, and other items, none of which seemed appropriate. Finally I settled on a jar of Ponds Cold Cream I was carrying. I could not imagine anyone checking the jar.

I took toilet tissue and carefully wrapped it around the pills before pushing it into the jar. I don't know why I used the tissue. I was trying to keep the pills from dissolving, yet the tissue would absorb moisture, causing the pills to deteriorate. Like so many other decisions, it was foolish yet, in my stress, seemed appropriate at the time. I slipped the small jar back inside my purse.

Descending toward Jose Martí airport, I watched the coastline of white sand beaches in the aquamarine sea. Tears came to my eyes. I started to panic. I had not taken any amphetamines that day in order for my mind to be clear. Had I done so, I would not have been so frightened. It was too late. What power, I wondered, was stronger, the CIA or a lover?

I had not told Fidel I was coming that day, though my earlier messages to his staff were such that they knew I would be arriving some time during the week. The CIA agents in

Havana had been correct about the planned television address, as well as the fact that he would be staying at the hotel instead of his home in Casa Cohimar twenty minutes away from Havana.

I was not as certain as they were of the evening that had yet to unfold. I knew Fidel was much less predictable than they believed. He would do whatever he felt like doing, and that meant I might not see him in the time alotted. I had only until my early evening return flight to kill him. The agency would be monitoring television from the University of Miami. If the address were cancelled, they would know I had succeeded.

I took a taxi to the Hotel Colina, a small hotel near the Hilton, where I booked a room for one day. I stayed only long enough to change into my uniform.

I checked the pills when I was inside my room at the Colina, discovering they had become soft and slightly mushy from the heat and the thick, wet cold cream. There was nothing I could do except hope I had not ruined them, that they would still dissolve without a trace.

Carrying my makeup case with me, I hailed a passing army Jeep to take me to the Hilton. Anyone in uniform could do that, a courtesy extended to the barbados who had fought with Fidel. I spotted our American agents on the sidewalk, playing drunk or eating fruit sold by vendors. They knew who I was, why I was there. Their actions were meant to be inconspicuous, to convince everyone they were tourists. Alex's word kept coming back to me, "Don't make God mad." I've never felt so alone.

I entered the Hilton lobby and I was home. I recognized the same woman at the desk in the lobby, the waiters working in the coffee shop. I smelled the coffee whose distinct aroma I had missed.

I took the elevator to the twenty-fourth floor, then used my key to enter the room. My heart was pounding. It felt so familiar. I checked to see if any women had been there. I looked for clothing, for bobby pins, for long blond hairs. To my relief, I didn't find anything.

The room was in Fidel's usual bachelor-style disarray. A bazooka was still under the bed sticking out. There were only two surprises. One was a pair of baby booties, which thrilled me though I did not let myself get sidetracked. The other was a new pair of custom-made British jodhpur boots with his name in gold on them.

Torn by feelings of love and obligation, I entered the bathroom. My emotions towards Fidel had never changed. Yet it had been made clear to me that, if I failed, there would probably be a war. I was made to feel responsible for any lives that might be lost. Yet I had no idea if I could kill him, would kill him. It all depended on Fidel. Alex's warning echoed in my head, "Do it."

I half expected the CIA to have an agent or a camera hiding in the bathroom. As usual, there was no shaving cream, no razor. It had been a joke between us. "I want to buy you aftershave, Fidel."

There was a towel crumpled on the floor. Typical. I touched it and found it was still wet. He had been there recently. He would probably be coming back before the speech.

I took out one of the pills. My hands were shaking as I tried to clean off the cold cream. It slipped, fell into the bidet. Then I took the other pill, still loaded with cream, and threw it with a splat into the bidet, flushing without looking to see if the pills went down.

Back in his room, there were piles of love letters, fan mail, and pictures from girls who told him that they wanted to meet the tall, handsome bachelor. I was enraged, not knowing if he had taken advantage of any of their offers. I drew faces on the pictures, adding mustaches, swastikas, and anything else I could think of. I tore up some of the steamier love letters, then tried to straighten the mess of ashtrays filled with cigar butts, toy tractors, the mismatched socks. The familiarity startled me. Looking out the window, past the balcony, at Havana, my fingers lingering on a cigar, its scent in my nostrils, I began to laugh. How utterly preposterous for me to be here to kill this man.

Fidel entered the room as though I had never left. He paused only briefly, then hugged me, said he was exhausted, that he needed sleep in order to give his talk that night.

Fidel had always been able to rest with me. He was endlessly tired from the constant pressure. Now he acted as though I had returned for good, and that meant that preparing for the speech was of greater importance than anything else. In his mind, I suspect, he thought we had the rest of our lives.

"I want to know about the baby," I told him. "I want to know now."

He asked if I came for him or to kill him. I told him both. But first I wanted to know about the baby.

"I know nothing," he frowned, looked concerned. "I had no part of that."

I said, "You're going to get killed twice. My father is going to kill you." Then, losing control, I began to cry. "I want to know what happened, Fidel."

Fidel explained that he had given no order, that the doctor had not acted on his behalf. He also said that the doctor had been executed for his actions.

Fidel became evasive about what happened to the baby.

"All boys born of Cuban fathers belong to Cuba," he told me.

And I replied, "I am the mother."

Fidel was too exhausted for prolonged talking. He tried to tell me about Cuba as it was developing under his changes. All I wanted to know about was our son, yet he would not discuss

8 1

that matter any further. Instead, he said he had to sleep, he could not go on without some rest. He laid down on the bed, closed his eyes, and said, "Did they send you to kill me?"

For a minute I didn't breathe, much less speak. I was completely taken aback, completely terrified.

The stub of a cigar was in his mouth. He was chewing it, an old habit.

"Yes, Fidel. They sent me to kill you."

Fidel closed his eyes. He reached for the large gun belt hanging over the lamp on the night stand beside the bed. I was frightened for a moment, knowing very well he could shoot me. It was what anyone in my position deserved. I also knew he wouldn't.

Fidel turned the .45 around, butt first, and held it out for me. His eyes were still closed as he said, "Take it."

I pressed the release, removing the ammunition clip of .45-caliber ammunition. He tensed at the sound, thinking I had retracted the hammer for firing, but he made no move to defend himself, to flee, or even to look at me.

"It's rusty," I said to him. "It needs oiling." I don't know why I said that. The gun was one he had carried throughout the revolution. It was important to him, custom-made with engraved pearl handles.

"Nobody, Marita," Fidel said sadly, "nobody can kill me." He turned his back to me.

"I will kill for the baby," I told Fidel, replacing the clip before tossing the gun on the bed by his leg. I walked to the foot of the bed and reached for his boots, untying the laces and removing them from his feet. His socks were still mixed up, still one black and one brown. At least this pair had no holes. In fact, they were new.

Room service had left us some coffee and sodas, and at his

request, I gave him one. He did not look to see if I put anything in it.

Fidel drank a Coke. I had a *café con leche*. He set down the bottle and patted the bed. We laid down together, hugging each other, kissing. In a few minutes we were naked and making love.

Killing him never entered my mind again. God! What a terrible waste it would be. Such dreams, such plans he had for Cuba.

Afterwards I went to the bidet and discovered that the pills were still there, floating on the surface. This time I flushed again and again and each time they popped up again. Finally, I mashed them up, they dissolved, and went down the drain.

Eventually I got down on my knees, hugging Fidel, begging him to let me see the baby. I told him that there was a hole in my heart that could only be filled by my holding our son.

Fidel was adamant. He loved me. He loved the boy. But I had to live with them in Cuba. "You think I don't understand your pain?" he asked, telling me my heart would heal if I would just stay.

Finally Fidel got dressed and left to prepare for the television address. I got up, looked through papers, pictures, gathering evidence to take to my CIA contacts. I knew it might be years before I saw my son. But I also knew that leaving was the best decision I could make, the only decision I could make. My employers would only come after me if I didn't. I wrote two letters, one to our son and one to Fidel, and placed them on the dresser. I kept $50 of the $6000 I had been given and stacked the rest with that letters on the dresser. The CIA never let me forget I gave that "Commie Bastard $6000 to get laid instead of killing him."

I decided to wear my uniform back to the United States, my act of defiance, and never bothered to check out of the Colina.

I was crying as I stepped outside the Hilton, hailed a taxi, and returned to the airport. Fidel had left by the bathers' elevator, unseen by the CIA agents. They spotted me, saw my tears, believed the job was finished, that my tears were out of remorse.

I was followed to the airport by the excited agents. They tried to signal their pleasure with what they were certain I had done. I did not acknowledge anything. I just wept silently, taking a long last look at the Cuba I loved.

The plane was delayed in leaving the airport. A little over forty minutes remained before the address was to begin. By the time the short flight to Miami was over, though, Fidel was well into his talk and the men who had sent me were livid.

Angrily I told those who had gathered to meet me, "I couldn't do it. It's your fucking war, not mine. I was crazy to go along with you."

I was taken out to the car with some of the members of the Sturgis-led special assassination squad, Operation 40, of which I was officially a part. The men who accompanied me were irate. They were especially appalled that I had returned in my uniform.

"I'm tired," I told them. "I want to take a shower, have a hamburger, go to sleep. I could have done it though—twice." I don't know why I added the smartass comment. Maybe to prove I was still in control over my life. I had reached my target like a good little hit lady. I had made him vulnerable. And I chose not to "whack" him. Besides, I was euphoric. My love had not been a dream. That was the ultimate power trip. I only wished my womb held his child to prove it.

"Oh, that's just great!"

"Twice," I said, trying to be bitchy. "I could have whacked him twice. He gave me his gun." Then, my voice softer, less defiant, I said, "But I couldn't do it." Alive, he would build hospitals and schools, but they didn't want to hear that.

"Jesus Christ. Our whole operation. Stupid bitch. God-damn, how are we going to answer to Washington?"

"Call them up and tell them to find somebody else," I said.

They called from the safe house. "She fucked it up," the agent yelled. "She blew it. She blew it. She's probably knocked up again. Dumb. Stupid. The bitch let us down."

Quietly I said, "I let my mother down, my father down, even myself. I'm tired. I just want to be alone."

And that was the end of it. Or so I thought.

I did not realize how wrong I could possibly be.

II

THE
SECOND
ASSASSINATION

1

I was told I'd have to work off the money spent on the assassination attempt. The pay back, however, would do little good in the course of history. Because I had failed to kill Fidel, he was going to murder every Marine on Guantanamo. The United States was going to be as overrun with Communists as abandoned waterfront buildings were overrun with rats. The Panama Canal was history, soon to be shut down by America's enemies. Russia would emerge triumphant, and all of Latin America would fall. The fate of the Western World had been in my hands, and I had used those hands for pleasure, not for death.

"We have inside information, Marita," I was told when I questioned the accuracy of their accusations. I thought Fidel had neither the interest nor the power to make such dramatic moves, but what did I know? They had better intelligence than I did. They were seemingly more objective than I was. They understood what I could not. Guatemala would need to become a new base for launching an assault, adding to the logistical difficulties of what would become the Bay of Pigs.

The Cuban leaders came by. The average soldier, the average pro-Batista man or woman in Miami, held a grudge against me. But the leaders had believed the story that Fidel killed my baby. They saw me as a troubled young woman, filled with love, hate, and grief. I had not been given the opportunity to mourn my murdered son. There were too many emotions to expect me to function effectively.

Frank Sturgis yelled at me. Frank Nelson was irate, as though I had personally betrayed him. There were young anti-Castro men who I thought might beat me. I was told the "American government" was irate, whatever that meant.

I felt guilty. I could not kill Fidel. Because I had failed to kill him, the men and women of the U.S. forces on Guantanamo were about to die. I watched the papers and listened to the news, waiting to hear the inevitable, to hear what I was responsible for causing. It did not happen.

I had been staying in a converted hotel safe house on Eighth Street in the Cuban community of Southwest Miami. The window of my room looked out on a field where I could see houses, birds, and the sky. It was neither pleasant nor unpleasant, but it was impossible to stay there for long without going stir crazy.

Finally I decided to take my chances. I had to return to some sort of normal life. I went out the front door, walked across the street to a small restaurant, and started talking with the waitress in Spanish. We established a friendship, so I told her that I needed a job.

I actually still had $500 from my work, but there was something wonderful about the chance to be a soda jerk or waitress, to live the life that everyone else lived. I got hired and did the work, proud of the tips I was earning. A week's pay and tips would never come to what I could make in a day or less doing jobs for Operation 40. But I didn't want to play in their dirty little war. I just wanted some peace.

I never did get the first week's paycheck. Sturgis and the others found me. "What are you doing here?" they demanded. "Get the fuck out of here. You're taking a boat."

I was making a milkshake when they slapped an envelope on the counter. I knew what the envelope contained. I knew it was stuffed with more money than I would ever receive for a "straight" job. I knew they were ridiculing what I was doing, reminding me that all of us were considered action whores, that we could be persuaded to do anything if the pay was right.

There was something terrible about that moment. I never was very good with math. I always had more money than I knew what to do with or less money than I needed because my commitments exceeded my resources. But I had learned how to make a good milkshake. I had learned how to make a hamburger and french fries and a hell of a delicious Dagwood Bumstead triple-decker sandwich. I understood that if I did a good job, I would go home each day with a pocket full of change. Sure, those who knew who I was—those Cubans who were aware that my mission had been to kill Castro and I had failed—refused to tip me. But everyone else treated me fairly, and I was proud to be a good waitress.

"Get the hell out," they told me. Then, pointing to my apron, they added, "Take that stupid thing off."

"They owe me money."

"Forget the fuckin' pay."

Being a waitress had been fun and challenging. Each day, and often well into the night, I had been in that coffee shop, feeding people, talking with them, accepting their scorn, their praise, or their indifference.

Yet I had become part of a radically different world, one that turned those normal societal values upside down. There the end justified the means, and the ends had whatever value we said they had. We were our own religion, our own gods. It was a world of no return. I felt I could never again stay in the midst of "normal" people. Sturgis and the rest were right on more levels than they realized. I could not stay in the coffee shop.

I was allowed to finish the night to help out the owner. Then I was driven to a house in Norman Key where I was expected to work off my debt by running guns and supplies for the anti-Castro Cubans.

No one talked with me as we drove. They talked with each other. They were determined to isolate me, to treat me as if I were dead, yet to use my skills.

2

I became one of the Operation 40 experts at gun running. Sometimes I took the load of guns directly to guerrilla fighters training on bases similar to ours in the Everglades. Other times I took them to locations such as the Bahamas where they would be off-loaded onto another boat for Central American destinations such as Guatemala or the Bahamas.

The base in Guatemala was to serve as one of the launching points for an attack against Castro. The country was friendly to the United States, hostile to Fidel, and willing to work with both the Attorney General's office and the CIA. That was why, a couple of years into the Kennedy administration, the government allowed Bobby Kennedy to declare New Orleans mob boss Carlos Marcello an illegal alien, deporting him to Guatemala on the pretense that the Tunis-born Italian citizen was somehow from that Central American country.

It was an exciting time for those of us involved with the transporting of arms. We stole the boats. We had men who went out "fishing" in the wealthy areas of Miami. They went in small boats, carrying rods and reels, as well as binoculars. They drifted along, observing the boats. My favorite was the thirty-six foot Chris-Craft, a perfect boat to gut and fill with guns and ammunition. Some of them were outfitted with every available luxury and worth hundreds of thousands of dollars.

Stealing a boat was actually quite easy. Once the appropriate boat was spotted, we returned on a night when there was little or no moonlight. We always picked a weekday when most people kept working hours and thus were not on the water as they might be over a weekend.

We used three boats and six people. They were equipped with outboard motors and oars, and rope so that they could be linked together for towing. We had wet suits and goggles, along with special equipment such as black paint and underwater cutting torches for slicing through the anchor chain.

One boat stayed at the base of the area where we were working. Two men were in that boat, using binoculars and a radio to alert us.

We rowed to the dock area. While the anchor chain for the selected boat was cut, one of us climbed the dock pole and either unscrewed the bulb or covered it with paint. Another person in a frog suit climbed onto the boat and freed the lines, enabling the rest of us to tow it. We tossed a grappling hook over the bow, made certain it was secure, and then all four of us went into the water, grabbing a line and pulling the boat.

Once we were away from the dock where it had been anchored and tied, we climbed on board, rolled up the rope, started the engine with either a master key or the picks of the man who was a lock expert. We removed our wet suit gear, put it in the hold, and then radioed the remaining two men that everything was fine.

I took the controls, moving us through the water, while the men in the fishing boat came for the two boats we had abandoned. They tied them together like a train, and rowed after us, starting their outboard when they were far enough away that the occupants of the waterfront houses would not become suspicious of the sound.

Even before we reached the designated landing point, we went through the equipment on board, seeing what we'd discard and what could be used. Special radio and weather gear, weapons, cash, or anything else that might help the cause were saved.

The mechanics who were waiting already had a blueprint of the stolen boat that had been targeted for theft. They had planned how to strip it, alter its appearance with paint, and prepare it for holding the maximum amount of arms and ammunition. They were ready to go to work, completing the task that night in order to move out the next day.

During the makeover, any personal items found on board were checked. Jewelry, if real, was taken for resale; I assume it was either moved through a known fence or altered so not to be identified. Clothing, personal papers, and anything similar was burned unless the mechanics wanted the items as bonus pay for their rapid, skillful work.

At first, everyone tried to ease my qualms about stealing the boats. I was told that money would be given to our victims in order to buy a vessel of identical size and quality.

The statement was not true, of course. No one could be permitted to know that CIA contract agents and pro-Batista soldiers were stealing boats for gun running. If an envelope filled with cash were suddenly on a victim's doorsteps, it would make headlines. There would be investigations by various law enforcement agencies and media reporters.

Many people were bribed by the contract agents, but they made their corruptibility obvious in advance. Most of our victims probably would not be influenced by cash. They would seek the truth, blow our cover, and have us all arrested.

MARITA

Someone stealing a boat could be understood. The vessel could be resold on the used yacht market anywhere in the world. Someone stealing a boat, then leaving an envelope with a couple of hundred thousand dollars was going to arouse suspicions no one wanted.

The other story I was told was that the owners went along. They were supposedly sympathizers with the cause. They wanted a larger boat, and since the stolen one was insured, they were delighted. In fact, they wanted us to blow it up after we were done with it so that they could be assured of keeping the money.

That story was easier to take. Still, I knew what was being said was nonsense. We blew up the boats or otherwise scuttled them after two or three runs because we dared not get caught.

Taking the boats became fun for me. I stopped thinking about the owners. They were rich. They could afford "toys" worth more than some people earned for a lifetime of work. The vessels were insured. I chose not to consider morals or ethics.

The law didn't matter. We were good at being boat thieves. We were never caught. Yet I always knew that if we got into trouble, a telephone call to the right person in Washington would eventually result in our release from any state or local jail. I was "Jane Bond," licensed to steal and do anything else I pleased. I was above the law, as were we all, and though we talked about the greater good we were doing for our country, we were destroying the essence of the Constitution.

Gun theft was less comfortable. It was a violent business. The armory guards were usually not bribed. They were trained defenders of valuable military property, and if given a chance, they would try to kill our people. We had to move swiftly, professionally, and, where necessary, violently.

Because I did not go inside, I pretended that no one was ever hurt, that at worst the guards were rendered unconscious.

I knew better. I went heavily armed for an armory job. I carried a .38 automatic snub-nosed detective special because it had solid killing power, a large capacity clip, and was accurate at a distance. I also carried a .25 caliber, semiautomatic handgun or a .22 revolver. And I had a razor-sharp, double-edged buck knife in one boot. I also had a .38 caliber short-barrel revolver if I needed a powerful weapon for close combat. I knew to shoot in the stomach to cause the victim's hand to relax, preventing my getting shot by a bullet fired by reflex at death. And I was skilled enough to shoot the person in the head, a certain kill, when there was no danger of a reflex action at the moment of death.

I did not show off how tough I was to the others. I intended to use my skills if I had to. I intended to get away alive and unhurt. I would take a life in an instant. I just did not wish to admit to the reality of my work any more than necessary.

We carried special equipment in our cars, including grappling hooks on ropes, thin nylon cord, flashlights, first-aid kits, a snakebite kit, emergency tents, water disinfectant pills, axes, water-repellent nets, hand grenades and dynamite, a cross bow and arrows, gags, duct tape, and flares. All the normal don't-leave-home-without-them necessities of your friendly neighborhood assassins. Naturally we had to worry about the trunk getting too hot during the daytime, since it was possible for the explosives to weep—become unstable—and go off prematurely.

My decoy work was easy. We parked the car away from the gate. The men I was with stayed hidden from view down the road. We also had additional cars needed for hauling explosives hidden out of sight; they were in position to move quickly. Only my car was obvious to the guards.

I walked up to the first guard station where an armed young man was on duty alone. As I caught his attention, the men with me moved as close as possible in order to be in the best position to jump him.

I normally wore a jumpsuit on these missions, but when I approached a guard I had on a pretty dress or attractive skirt and blouse, my dog tags hidden from view. I smiled, flirted with him, sometimes pretending to be a single woman, and at other times to be a single mother with a baby in the car. Whatever my story, I always claimed the car had broken down, and I always made certain the guard felt that I was sexually attracted to him.

I insisted that the perimeter guard be chloroformed so he wasn't harmed. He was caught by surprise and never had a chance to resist.

Once the guard was subdued, his hands and feet were securely tied, he was gagged, then dragged out of the way. The men went over the gate while I stayed near the loading area.

We usually had ten to fifteen men on such a mission, the cars serving as a caravan. They went inside and subdued or bribed any guards who got in their way. Some ended locked in rooms, restrained, or otherwise safely incapacitated.

Armory thefts were not Frank's specialty. They are much more common than people think. The government seldom reports them to the media. When reports leak out, the government makes sure that the barest minimum of details are released to the press. Numerous terrorist groups, political extremists, and others know that armories are where the surplus military supplies are. They also know that some armory personnel can be bought or effectively threatened. Some are not dedicated career officers but two-year enlistees who don't give a damn if someone takes some rifles, handguns, bazookas, or the more recent lightweight anti-tank weapons. They get paid well for looking the other way. Or they get double-crossed, sometimes killed, sometimes hurt, and other times left bound, gagged, and penniless. After all, who are they going to tell that they were willing to sell out their country for what, to us, was chump pocket change?

After getting access to the weapons, the men divided into teams. It took two men to carry a case of rifles, for example. Moving quickly, it was possible to steal at least a couple hundred weapons. These were placed in the cars, usually stripped of cases so they would fit more easily in every available space.

Finally we rode out in a caravan, traveling the back roads to avoid local sheriff's deputies and police. Our cars were low to the ground, their suspensions strained, the tires stressed beyond the loads they had been built to handle.

Sometimes we encountered aging bridges that did not appear capable of handling the load. Usually the drivers backed each car down the road then floored the engine, using the extra distance for better momentum. Sometimes we raced across the bridge. Sometimes the angle of the road and bridge were such that we rose slightly off the ground, slamming down hard.

We joked about the possibility that some of the weapons might explode. They didn't. At least not in the caravans of which I was a part. But we were always nervous, and frequently we blew a tire and had to stop to replace it.

We did buy some military equipment, including used B-25 aircraft used to transport supplies and to drop leaflets over Cuba. Frank Sturgis was a good pilot, and the leaflets were meant for propaganda. We used crop dusting planes and landing strips and similarly poor quality runways.

The leaflets were prepared 500 to a bundle. They were tied with strings in such a way that we could drop the bundle, holding on to the string, the leaflets fluttering down like snowflakes in the wind.

During quiet times I helped prepare the bundles. However,

bored with such work and eager for mischief, I added as many notes as I could without someone seeing me. I wrote, "Fidel, I love you" on some of the leaflets; "Love, Marita" or "Viva Cuba!" on others. I even wrote "Don't believe it" on a few. Either no one discovered what I was doing or no one minded. We had to justify buying the airplanes, and while leaflets had no impact on the people, they were a way for us to justify the money being spent.

3

Towards the end of 1960, the CIA-sponsored operatives became convinced they were going to be launching their invasion at any moment. I was to be in the first group to strike. In a convoy with 500 men, I went into the Everglades for a month of intensified training. We had constant driving rainfall, mosquitoes, and bullshit tests of bravery to prepare us for the overthrow of the Castro government.

Frank Sturgis wanted to learn which of us had "the biggest balls." We were about to go into warfare. We would have knowledge that was desired by Castro's men. It was important to learn who had courage and who might break under pressure before we went down.

For example, Sturgis brought a burlap bag tied securely with rope around the opening. He took it from his truck, hung it from a tree, and had twenty-five of us line up.

Sturgis announced that the bag was filled with rattlesnakes.

He said that each of us was to go to the bag and jam a hand inside for a count of three. Then we were to remove our hand and go on to the next activity, a parachute jump. Those who failed this test of nerves would be sent "back up north," meaning to Miami. Given the enthusiasm of the Cuban community for what we were doing, such a return would have resulted in widespread ridicule and ostracism.

The soldiers were all ages, from eighteen or nineteen years old to late fifties. They were all bragging about what they were going to do, but they were scared.

I was the fifth or sixth one in line. I went to the bag, coolly looked at the man standing by with a snake bite kit, then thrust my hand into the bag where I could hear their tails. I wasn't bitten.

The truth was that I almost shit in my pants I was so terrified. I didn't care if the antivenom in the kit would keep me from dying. I was almost out of control from fright. However, I remembered the training I had been receiving and decided to use it against Sturgis and the others. I showed no emotion, not when I looked at the Op with the snake bite kit, not when I heard the warning rattles as I stuck my hand into the bag, and not while I endured the count before I could remove my hand. I was the only woman Op. I just had to be the best.

Amazingly, only two of the boy soldiers were bitten. One was seriously ill for several days. The other was sent back to Miami.

While we were going through this training, some of the group was periodically sent into Cuba on special extended missions. For example, when the sugar cane crop was a good one, the CIA deliberately arranged for at least some of it to be destroyed so Castro would lose a source of revenue, an action both intensely cruel and brilliant. Covert agents, usually a brigade member, would sneak into Cuba, then take a cat to the fields. He would tie a kerosene soaked rag to the cat's tail. Then the rag would be set ablaze. The terrified, tortured cat ran crazily through the sugar cane, trying to flee the fire. The burning rag set the cane ablaze, often ruining thousands of acres.

The cat trick was so successful that it has been repeated over the years, even to the present day. Fidel protested before the United Nations, but it did no good. Dry sugar cane burns readily, and this technique is simple and effective. The viciousness required to think up such an action reveals a great deal about the men with whom I was working.

It was a very dirty covert war filled with vengeance, hate, and greed.

Frank Sturgis was our military advisor. Our group, Brigade 2506 (later Alpha 66 and Omega 7), contained Op 40, the assassination squad of which I was a member. There were about 25 of us, full–time CIA employees or contract employees, in Op 40.

Another group was led by Rolando Masferrer, a former Cuban Senator known as El Tigre. Its members had all worked for Batista in some capacity. They had been the greedy, sadistic rogues of the old regime, the violent, brutal men who kept order. They enjoyed hurting others. There was great hostility between Sturgis and Masferrer.

There was much more taking place in the way we were being trained than I realized. There was a subtle combination of created rivalry and group bonding. We took pride in how we handled ourselves relative to the others. I was able to endure weather extremes better than the average hot-headed male brigade member. I was one of the few who never collapsed while carrying a 100-pound pack on forced marches in the Everglades. And I was a better handgun and rifle shot than almost anyone.

The idea was to get us comfortable with an action we might not take on our own, yet we would not hesitate to take as part of the group. I could not deliberately and in cold blood take a life

103

on my own, as they had seen with Castro. Yet if I was part of a team, I was expected to shoot first and have remorse later. In hindsight, God help me, I think they were right.

The work I was doing was financially rewarding, but offered few other benefits. Once a month I received an envelope filled with cash from "Eduardo." I wanted for nothing, did not worry about taxes, food, shelter, or clothing. I earned more than I needed, more than I wanted. I put aside all sense of femininity, all desire to date, have sex, marry, or lead a normal life. I was able to act out my anger in ways other people merely fantasize about, not realizing how quickly such dreams can turn to nightmares. And I was respected by some of the toughest, most dedicated fanatics ever assembled for covert operations from American soil.

Frequently the only woman with 500 men, I was sexually tested, of course. During one of the weapons-testing sessions in the Everglades when we had to live and work together day and night in mosquito-ridden swamps, the men made one too many sexual cracks. I grabbed an M-1 rifle, jumped onto a truck, and fired a round in the air to get their attention. "Okay," I shouted. "I don't give a damn if you hate your mother, girlfriend, sister. I'm going to sleep here tonight, and you come near me, I'll kill you instantly." Was I serious? Neither they nor I wanted to find out. I was left alone after that.

The immense tension over my presence in the Everglades that lingered had less to do with my being a woman than with my being a failed assassin.

My failure to kill Fidel had often been compared to U2 pilot Gary Francis Powers' failure to kill himself with a poison-tipped needle when his plane was shot down over Russia in 1960. He was treated horribly by the CIA when he was finally released, and I never believed that his death was an accident. I always identified with him. It made me more than a little insecure about my own life expectancy. Armed, trained men blamed me for not fulfilling the mission that would take them from the swamps and allow them to return to Havana. One of them actively wanted to hurt me.

The incident occurred when we were test firing and learning to handle new weapons effectively. We were shooting at targets placed different distances away. In addition, some of the men were experimenting with the new C-4 explosive, a puttylike substance that could be shaped and hidden in almost anything. Explosions and the sound of rifle fire were everywhere.

Suddenly I felt as though I had been pushed hard against my neck. I heard someone cry "Medic" before I realized I was bleeding. I had no pain, but I did have a flesh wound through my neck. It was bleeding as I stood up, the blood pouring down my back.

I went over to a Jeep to sit down. One of the men tried using first aid, though nothing staunched the blood. When the initial shock of the wound also wore off, I began to feel the pain. It was so intense that it seemed to fill my body.

I had to return to Miami for help because the dressing on my wound would not stop the bleeding. Only a single truck went to Miami, and then not until nightfall. One person, especially a failed assassin, did not warrant a special trip. I would have to wait, which I did, becoming ill from the growing pain, the shock, and the blood loss.

I was taken to the home of Dr. Orlando Bosch, a physician who had switched from being a pediatrician to being a terrorist. He eventually served jail time for involvement in the bombing of a Cuban airliner that exploded with extensive loss of life. A hospital would have had to make out a police report. Dr. Bosch was legally obligated to do so, as a part of Operation 40, he, too, was above the law.

105

MARITA

We got away with gun running, killing, and theft. There were times when we were stopped by local law enforcement authorities. It happened to me a couple of times with a truck convoy of weapons, and it happened to others. Each time the local police were told to call a certain telephone number. I never knew exactly who was reached, but I did know that we were immediately let go. The incident simply had not happened, the police had seen nothing. Bosch was protected like the rest of us. It was even easier to hide a wound than it was to hide corpses.

I was patched up and watched for two days in the house. There was no suturing done, though the bleeding was stopped. Unfortunately the first aid had been inadequate against infection, and I became quite ill. The wound, just below the ear in the neck, had to be reopened, cleaned of infection, and closed. Once I became well enough, I returned to the motel that served as our safe house.

Nothing was right when I went back. I had lost my taste for playing war. I spent much of my time either in the room or in the lobby, cleaning guns. Late at night, the young soldiers would travel back and forth to the Everglades for maneuvers, always moving at an hour when they would not be spotted. I hated everything that was happening, but there was no way out.

4

I had to heal before going back into the field, so in June 1961 I became a part of a new mission, this one nonviolent. Miami was the home for a number of wealthy Latin Americans who had to leave their countries for one reason or another. Some were members of privileged families who fled during a political coup. Some were high officials who embezzled or accepted bribes long enough to amass a fortune, allowing them to leave and live in comfort for the rest of their lives. And some were losers in political fights, deposed dictators, defeated military leaders. Many changed their names. Others tried to keep a low profile. Some who were wealthly enough liked to play power politics by financing those who might do their revenge for them. Among the latter was Marcos Pérez Jiménez, the deposed dictator of Venezuela and enemy of Fidel Castro.

Frank Sturgis came to me and told me that I was going to go see one of these wealthy expatriates, a man named General Diaz. I was given an address in Miami Beach, and told to clean up, put on some makeup, and "look like a girl."

This was the first time I had been asked to go on what were

actually fund-raising missions. These were regular visits to the wealthy and powerful to solicit money beyond what the CIA was supplying. The money was never really necessary. The CIA funds more than paid for the war games we were playing. Soliciting funds let donors feel they were part of an important cause. They liked throwing parties and having real revolutionaries in their midst to titillate them with stories of violence and heroics, some of which may actually have happened.

It might have been called "guerrilla chic," a situation similiar to "radical chic" in Manhattan when the "in" thing was to have Black Panthers mingling with wealthy white socialites. Giving a few thousand dollars to our cause was just another expense for an exciting evening, like paying the caterer and the musicians.

The mercenaries who led us and the more corrupt members of the Cuban community understood this and took advantage of it. They went collecting the same way people seek donations to fight cancer or heart disease. One difference was that they traveled armed.

I wasn't sure why I was being asked to be a courier, to play bag lady to some rich sucker. Probably, I was still being punished for having failed to kill Fidel.

I wore a frilly white blouse that showed off my figure. I carried no identification in case anyone stopped me. I carried an empty bag I later found I did not need. I had a .38-caliber, short-barreled revolver in my back pocket. Just another late adolescent out on the town.

The house on Pine Tree Drive was your basic Miami Beach mansion. It had twelve-foot electric fortified gates. There was an ocean-going yacht bobbing on the Indian River behind the house. Floodlights illuminated a beautifully landscaped garden. Expensive cars lined the driveway. Seven security men made certain that only invited guests enjoyed the music and elaborate food.

I was expected. One of the guards took me to a short, bald, overweight man who seemed slightly nearsighted as he squinted his gray eyes and studied me closely, smiling. I was told he was "Mr. Diaz," and I assumed that his military history was the reason he was no longer in his native country.

Mr. Diaz took me into an elegant room that was obviously a reception area. A map of Venezuela was on the wall; the furnishings were expensive. Then he told me to wait. He left and returned with a bottle of fine Rhine wine and a gym bag holding two or three hundred thousand dollars in cash.

The Rhine wine was for me. The money, he said, was just "a little something for rice and beans for the cause."

I thanked him, and he replied, "It's nothing. A little help to get rid of your old boyfriend."

I set the bag down.

"How dare you. Keep this." I turned and began to walk out.

He ran after me, calling, "No, no, please. I'm sorry. I didn't mean to offend you."

I resented the remark. He obviously knew my history in a way that would only come from Frank or the other brigade leaders. I didn't know who he was, other than that he was some bigwig. I also did not appreciate it when he asked me to dinner.

"Mr. Diaz" seemed to have some special connection with Sturgis and the rest. He knew about the safe-house motel where I was living. He knew my schedule. When I wasn't in the Everglades, he regularly pursued me in his white Mercedes, stopping me to ask if I would have dinner with him.

The first time he came to see me, I was sitting just outside the safe-house motel cleaning a rifle. I was near a back drive that was never used by outsiders so no one would be shocked by what I was doing. I was dressed in fatigues and had dirt under my fingernails. It was just two days after I picked up the cash, and by then I had learned that the home I visited was next door to the estate once owned by Al Capone.

The driver informed me, "The general would like to speak with you."

I brushed him off, rudely replying, "After the war, maybe."

Four days later I received a heavy eighteen-carat gold bracelet with a coin bearing his picture. When it first arrived I was too busy working to bother with it. After I had a chance to study it later that night, I realized that the coin had been made by the Venezuelan mint and that the general was an extremely important man.

Everywhere I went, his little red and white Mercedes sports coup showed up. Finally, the general returned in person, I commented on the coin. He said that the coin was actually one that had been minted as a commemorative of his coming to power. There were only five in existence, and I now owned one. He said I should feel honored.

I did feel honored by his persistence. After a few weeks I told "General Diaz" to return in an hour. I would go out with him.

The dinner was not so enjoyable an evening as it might have been. He considered it a private affair, romantic and peaceful. The restaurant was expensive, elegant. But I was troubled by the fact that we were not alone. Armed guards sat all around, tense, ever vigilant. Finally he admitted that Diaz was not his real name. He was General Marcos Pérez Jiménez, the former president of Venezuela, who had been forced from his country in 1958. The new government under Rómulo Betancourt had been trying to extradite him from Miami ever since. He had gotten caught on his way into exile with a suitcase filled with Jockey shorts and $13 million in cash. He was also wanted for murder. He told me he was sort of like Fidel, only nicer. Fortunately, he could not read my thoughts.

Marcos had systematically looted the country of at least $750 million. The money was carefully hidden in banks, real estate, and various businesses and corporations throughout the world. No matter where he had fled, he could afford to live in luxury, always buying the loyalty of as many armed guards as he needed to stay alive. For now, he wasn't supposed to leave the confines of Dade County and had to check in once a month at INS, the Immigration and Naturalization Service.

I later learned the type of ruler he had been. Marcos, assisted by his loyal Chief of Police, Pedro Estrada, was willing to do anything necessary to stay in power. Enemies were routinely murdered. Suspected enemies were tortured, and if they did not confess their crimes, they, too, were killed. The innocents who seemed a threat were merely jailed, their bodies shattered by the time they were allowed to walk or be carried from prison.

While President of Venezuela, Marcos arranged to receive a percentage of every American business in his country. Money was spread around to the handful of wealthy, powerful families who supported him while the peasants became poorer and hated him. He also did whatever the CIA asked of him, figuring that was a way to keep the Americans happy

All this knowledge did not come until later. All I knew at first was that a former Venezuelan leader in exile, who used some of his wealth to finance the anti-Castro movement, was courting me. I was flattered, and though I resented his comparing himself to Fidel and inquiring into my private life, I began to accept more of his invitations. Certainly it was better than constantly preparing for war, the only alternative I felt I had at the time.

During the period of my recovery, my wound prevented me

from returning to the field. I was unable to carry heavy packs, so I couldn't participate in maneuvers in the Everglades. I began going out with Marcos regularly. Before long I decided the time was right to leave the safe house and accept a position as a stewardess for Pan American Airways. They were hiring young women with language skills and were pleased to have me because I was fluent in several languages. I signed on and was given six weeks of paid training.

Being with Pan Am meant I could collect a paycheck and lead a normal life. I would be earning my living in a way I could admit to. I could travel. I could return to Europe to see Papa. My first assignment was to be the Latin American division. I assumed my absence wouldn't cause much concern in the Everglades. What I didn't count on was Marcos having me fired.

Marcos never told me he was upset when I joined Pan Am, perhaps because I was so pleased. He had talked about renting an apartment for me, and I accepted the idea. We were intimate by then, but I didn't know if the relationship would last. I didn't know if anything would last in my life other than the job I had gotten on my own. I intended to pay for the apartment from the money I earned, so I would be independent. If I got into a bind, I had already made friends with a stewardess who could be my roommate.

Marcos took me to see the apartment he had selected for me. I was expecting something modest. He owned a lot of land, apartment buildings, and houses in Miami. Real estate was a good way to hide large sums of money back then. He made money on the rents. The property could be resold easily, and ownership could be kept fairly secret. A number of dictators were making such investments in the United States, as were members of organized crime. Some of the buildings were luxurious. Others catered to middle-income families. I figured he would put me into one of his lower priced buildings, then give me a discount on the lease. Instead he took me to Surfside Drive, an elegant new housing development tucked away under palm trees on North Miami Beach. A pontoon bridge passed over a waterway. The setting was idyllic and expensive.

Marcos took me to an unattached, two-story duplex in this development. He had the key. He had paid the rent for a year. It was so luxurious the lease must have cost more than I was making with the airline, probably more than I could ever hope to make.

He took me through. The dwelling came with furnishings to match the cost of the surroundings. It was a modern home, with state-of-the-art appliances in the oversized kitchen, pastel colors throughout, and a feeling of quiet that assured those wealthy enough to afford it a mental and physical escape from nearby Miami Beach. It was a location where the rich could raise a family in safety and privacy, and where the wealthy elderly could reflect on the success that enabled them to end their days with such pleasure.

We went through the sliding glass doors in back, then walked down to the dock that would allow his thirty-eight-foot Chris-Craft yacht to be docked. ("Great," I thought the first time I saw it, "at least this one I won't have to swipe.") The channel was deep and connected to the Indian River waterways. He could sail over at any time, coming in the back way.

For a moment I wasn't certain what to do. I had my job with Pan Am and no place to live. I had come to like Marcos, at least as I knew him in Miami. His past did not bother me because it did not affect our relationship. My past had already caught up with me. I was both respected and hated in the Everglades, and someone had shot me. I decided to agree to what I, at first, considered a business arrangement born of necessity.

113

I would be Marcos' official mistress, a not unpleasant thought. I enjoyed his company. He planned to spend most of his time with me, though it was obvious that he would not divorce his wife. He had considered bringing me into his home on Pine Tree Drive since his wife lived in Lima, Peru, most of the time, but she visited him often enough that he could not risk my being there. Instead, he would use my place and our relationship to relax in a way he had not been able to do previously. He also planned to change his life, to enter, at least for the immediate future, into a relationship that was committed.

From what I later learned, I think there were two reasons for what he did. The first was that he wanted to take control of me, to make me his lover so he could have me when Fidel could not. Marcos hated Fidel.

Fidel loved me. I have never doubted that. Marcos found me sexually exciting and enjoyed my company, but also liked the idea of humiliating his enemy by having sex with the woman he loved. He made certain Fidel knew. He even occasionally asked me if he were better in bed than Fidel, a question I resented.

The other reason was one I did not want to think about, though I knew he was right. One evening over dinner he said to me, "Am I your next assignment or are you mine?"

I was startled by the question and asked him what he meant. Marcos told me he felt that at least some of the Cuban exile leaders and CIA covert operatives wanted one or both of us dead. He felt that my being shot was no accident.

"You failed your mission with your lover Fidel," he said, "and they want to kill you." The shot might have been a warning. It might have been a way to cause me pain. And it might have been an assassination attempt that did not allow for a second round to be fired because the second round would have called attention to the shooter. Marcos would keep me alive, he promised. He would keep me safe from the CIA and the Cubans. He had the money to buy loyal guards. He had property. He had access to weapons well beyond what I always carried. I could stop playing war.

My flying off to be a stewardess for Pan Am was simply not consistent with his plans. Like a pesky mosquito, they were terminated.

During the time Marcos was in power, he had never been able to enjoy being a father. He had married and sired children, but he had no part in rearing them. He had never changed a diaper. He had never fed his children. He let his staff handle anything routine or unpleasant, spending time with his family when he felt like using them for recreation.

The relationship with his wife was similarly distant. Sex with his wife was a duty. In Latin America, a mistress is for physical pleasure, but enjoys the privileges of a wife. Both are compatible so long as neither objects to the arrangement each knows to exist.

For both religious and financial reasons, Marcos would not divorce his wife. In their world, it was natural for them to stay together. She had wealth, servants, every luxury she might desire. He did not flaunt his mistresses or embarrass her with his intimate activities.

Marcos had played with a wide variety of women. He was ready for a change. He wanted, at least for a short period of time, a real family with which he could be involved. I was the key to that end for him.

5

I was delighted with the house. I agreed to the arrangement, and Marcos arranged a celebration of our new status in our new home. I thought it was a house warming. He and his friends considered it a formal announcement of my becoming the general's mistress. The only difference between the event and a wedding reception was that there would be no wedding ceremony preceding it.

It was an odd evening. The happy couple was feted and toasted by almost fifty men on Marcos' birthday. We had caviar, sparkling wine, and elaborately prepared food. Among the delighted celebrants was Pedro Estrada, the former chief of the Venezuelan secret police and long time aide to Marcos. He was a shifty-eyed bastard whose pleasures in life had been torture and death. He was a student of the most extreme tactics used by the Nazis in the death camps, adapting the more hideous methods for his own. He was totally loyal to Marcos, and thus respectful to me.

I did not fully understand how important the celebration was until Marcos gave me a special seal of his love. He had been an officer in Peru at one time, and had received a ring after graduating from military academy. He slipped the ring from his finger and placed it on my own, a sign to all his followers that I was to be treated with greater respect than his wife. It was also the final, visible sign that I was his possession.

I was unsure exactly what was in store for me. I wondered if the large number of men would remain in the house. I wondered what our life style would be.

I only had my relationship with Fidel by which to compare what was taking place. Life with Fidel in the Havana Hilton had been full of excitement, not too different from the life I enjoyed on Papa's ship. Now I had a large, beautifully furnished house equipped with the latest electronic surveillance equipment, bodyguards—Sabas, Briceños, Raúl who were always heavily armed—a state-of-the-art music system complete with all the Venezuelan records Marcos could find, and a frilly white canopy bed to share with a dictator. I didn't know if men such as Pedro Estrada would be living there. I didn't know what was expected of me. I didn't even have appropriate clothing. Marcos insisted I buy everything new.

Marcos moved his own clothing and personal possessions into the house, making it clear that he now considered this his second residence. Then he bought me a car, a new Thunderbird, so that both of us could come and go without anyone spotting his Mercedes.

It should have been the beginning of an idyllic life. I would finish my training with Pan Am and begin flying throughout Latin America. I might go to school in my spare time.

The truth was quite different. Marcos arranged for me to be fired from Pan Am. I had passed my training with high grades. I met all their requirements and should have gone on my first assignment. But Marcos wanted me totally under his control, available for him at all times. I would not be working.

Meanwhile my unexpected pregnancy became evident. It would have marked the end of my career anyway. What are today called "flight attendants" were always single females back then. They never were pregnant. And if they secretly married, they never wore their rings on the job. They were trained experts in survival, on board to save lives in the event of an air disaster. But the public image was that of the "sky waitress" who was an easy target for those lucky few who asked in the right way. The public had to be diverted from thinking about the worst-case scenarios for which we were trained.

I was working in a mock-up of a galley, practicing making coffee in the giant urns they used, when I suddenly felt nauseous. It was my first sign of morning sickness, though I did not realize that fact, even after similar incidents began occurring with some frequency.

Finally Marcos sent me to Dr. Harry E. Wolk, a respected gynecologist, to be checked. I did not know what was wrong. It never occurred to me I was pregnant. I had been assured I was sterile as a result of what happened to me in Cuba. The trouble was that no one explained this anti-Castro propaganda to my perfectly healthy woman's body for which unprotected sex still meant pregnancy.

The baby was already six weeks old so there was no question about the diagnosis. I told Marcos, not knowing what to expect his reaction to be, and was surprised by his delight. He wanted to have a son since he already had four daughters. But whatever we had, he was thrilled.

This baby Marcos and I were going to rear. He was going to be a daddy. He was going to change diapers, feed the baby, walk the floor, and do whatever else had to be done. Maids had raised his four daughters. This time it was his turn.

Marcos followed every superstition he had ever heard about ensuring a healthy baby. He brought home cases of smoked mussels and other food supposed to promote fetal development. He made certain I had good care and comfortable surroundings. He spent extensive time with me. When I wasn't with him, I was going to the beauty parlor, the store, the movie theater. He arranged for a wonderful nanny named Willy May Taylor to be my companion, help with the baby, and generally make my life more comfortable. We also found a reliable babysitter, Mrs. Lillian Green.

Despite Marcos' joy, our relationship was quite volatile. He was set in his ways, not a man to reform overnight, and both of us had quick tempers.

For example, Marcos' Chris-Craft could sleep six people, was stocked with expensive liquor, caviar, and other delights, and frequently was used for entertaining. He had long enjoyed taking military leaders on his yacht, hiring some beautiful Cuban prostitutes, and letting them all have a good time—these were his "business affairs." I warned him that I didn't care about his past, however, so long as we were together, he was going to be faithful to me. The yacht was no longer to be used for what amounted to floating orgies.

One night I knew he would be returning from his island, Soldier's Key, with a boatload of intoxicated business men and curvy Cuban women, I grabbed my .38 and waited for him at the dock, hiding inside another boat. I intended to grab him, threaten him at gunpoint, let him know that I was serious about my demands. The water was choppy and the boat was moving so much that my first round hit metal, ricocheted, and struck him in the knee. He realized that if I had killed him at that moment, I would have had no regrets. That was the last time he was unfaithful in any way.

That was not the only time I lost my temper with him. He frequently drank too much at dinner, and when he got drunk he would make a fool of himself. He sometimes called Rómulo

Betancourt, the man who took power from him in Venezuela, threatening his life and calling him Pato-Pato. Marcos had long gotten a fee for every oil tanker leaving Venezuela, and during one of the telephone conversations, he warned his successor that he was going to blow up one of the ships. He liked harassing Betancourt by reminding him of his continuing power even in exile and promising one day he'd return.

Marcos also called Fidel, mocking him because Castro had neither wealth nor the woman who had been so important to him. The calls were undoubtedly recorded by the State Department or others, and complaints about them from some of the allies he threatened endangered Latin American/U.S. relations. The FBI had to step in and ask him to stop. He would not listen, which was held against him during the effort to extradite him back to Venezuela.

I handled him my own way. Marcos was always a practical joker. Once, when I was suspicious that he had been unfaithful, he passed out drunk after making a fool of himself. I got some adhesive tape and taped up his penis. Then I went to sleep. In the morning Marcos awakened and started to scream. I told him I would use alcohol to remove the adhesive, but when I applied it, he started bellowing to the guards I was trying to assassinate him. "How can such a small penis hurt so much?" I asked him, delighting in his discomfort. Finally, I rescued him from his misery, having him sit in a bathtub filled with hot water, and bubble bath, and the adhesive loosened quickly and simply.

Two weeks into my ninth month, I called my mother in Ft. Lee, New Jersey. I didn't want to shock her, so I spoke to my brother Joe, a foreign service officer who was about to be transferred to the U.S. Embassy in Argentina.

"Jo-Jo," I stammered, "I'm having a baby in two weeks."

Silence. "WHAT?"

When I said who the father was, I heard, "Oh my God, no, not another dictator, no, not the terrible General Marcos Peréz Jiménez, the brutal killer?"

Silence. "Yes. Please tell Mama. I'll be up tomorrow."

Both Joe and my mother were horrified.

Marcos agreed I could have the baby in New Jersey, as long as I was kept under guard. I flew up with four guards, $10,000 cash, and a gold and diamond pin for my mother.

Marcos called daily. Mama wasn't pleased to have another dictator in the family, but chatted with him for hours, picking on him mercilessly.

Mama pampered me, set up a nursery, knitted, and teased the guards who kept saying "the little general will never come."

Marcos wanted a boy. I wanted a girl. Dictator fathers, in my experience, tended to take over boy babies. This baby was to be mine. Nobody was going to get her away from me.

February 27th, the due date, passed.

Labor started on March 8th, at the end of a furious snowstorm. I had to be taken to New York Lying-In Hospital in a Fort Lee police car by a brave rookie. At six A.M. on March 9, 1962, my absolutely perfect and beautiful baby daughter, came into the world weighing 8 lbs. 2 oz. My very own baby, her little fingers and toes perfect, her round face and bowknot mouth the spitting image of Marcos. She was the exact stamp of her papa, only she had long black straight hair. Marcos was almost bald.

When the guards handed me the phone to tell Marcos he had a beautiful baby girl, he said, "What? Not a boy?" He wanted to name her Adela Maria after his mother. I named her Monica Mercedes Pérez Jiménez. After two weeks, I returned to Miami.

Before I left New Jersey, Marcos set up a trust fund for $75,000 for baby Monica. Marcos' and my attorney was former Justice Department official David W. Walters, of Walters, Moore and Costanzo law firm, in the Ainsley Building, Miami. He was also the trustee and handled everything. The funds were in the form of stocks, bonds and debentures in the First National Bank of Miami. The trust was "irrevocably and unconditionally" Monica's. Since Marcos was married, he was referred to anonymously as the "Grantor" of the trust fund.

Marcos was amazed when I handed him our new-born daughter. He gently held her, counted her fingers and toes, laughed at her mouth, so much like his. He changed her diapers, spoon-fed her, slept with her, took her everywhere.

He even went so far as to have a custom-made crash helmet prepared for Monica so she could ride about Miami in his sports car.

Monica was a beautiful child. Pedro Estrada nicknamed her "The Little General" because she looked like an attractive version of Marcos. The advertising agency handling the Beech-Nut baby food account wanted Monica to be in their ads. That could not be allowed, though, because Marcos would not tolerate the agency having the address and other information they routinely required. He wanted his daughter protected from danger.

Marcos was right. Not long after returning to Miami, Monica was grabbed from Willy May while she was on the telephone. Fortunately ransom was demanded and paid almost immediately. Saving Monica cost $300,000.

The next few weeks were filled with joy and confusion. Papa blamed Marcos for getting me pregnant and not marrying me. "I have a good mind to come down and shoot your balls off," he told Marcos during one irate telephone call. However, when he saw Monica, his first known grandchild, he cried. He no longer cared how the child had been conceived. What mattered to him was that she existed. Still, a little frustrated, he said to me, "You do everything backwards."

6

On December 12, 1962, Marcos was taken to the Dade County jail. U.S. Attorney General Robert Kennedy, Secretary of State Dean Rusk, Supreme Court Justice Arthur Goldberg, Rómulo Betancourt, and others had worked out a deal in which he would be deported to Venezuela. The Venezuelans had formally indicted him for the theft of the $13 million he had tried to smuggle on his last trip out of the country. All of his various and enormous payoffs to law enforcement officials and politicians didn't prevent Federal marshals, Customs, and INS officials from taking him out of bed and incarcerating him.

Months passed. Marcos was charged $200 cash a day by Dade County jail guards to use the phone to call me. He lost forty pounds. He had an August deadline to be returned to Venezuela. His wife and three daughters went to Lima, Peru; the eldest daughter eloped to Key West.

The U.S. Border Patrol boarded up the windows to Marcos' $400,000 + estate. His personal possessions, including his eleven cars, were shipped to Peru. Gone were the posh parties, the $2000 + a month electric bill for floodlights alone. Visible today still are the high gates, large trees, and driveway, but the buildings have been removed to lower property tax. A corporation in which Marcos' attorney, David Walters, is an officer now owns the property.

Time was running out. All legal tactics were exhausted. Marcos said the most effective way to stall the departure was for me to sue him for paternity.

"But I can't do that, Marcos," I said. "I'll get publicity. It will hit the papers and violate the trust fund." (Marcos was the "Grantor"; if I revealed his name, the trust would be terminated.)

Marcos said not to worry.

I stalled. We discussed it for days. He said it was the only way to save him, to keep him in the country. I reluctantly agreed. I got an attorney. Papers were prepared and filed. Marcos was depressed that Monica would have to be used as a legal maneuver.

Upon filing, I hit the front page of the papers.

I hid in my apartment. Two of Bobby Kennedy's personal advisers came to visit me. They demanded that I fully drop the paternity suit. They said I was "obstructing justice," "interfering with international judicial procedure," and that Washington was very upset.

I told them my suit was a civil suit and I wouldn't drop it.

"Look, Lorenz," one of them said, "the U.S. government will make good the trust fund, tax free."

In the paternity suit, with Marcos' approval, I had filed for five million dollars.

The two men were angry when I said no deal. They said I could very well end up in jail next to my fat boyfriend, the dictator. I said it was un-American to threaten a pregnant mother, one who had served the country in the Bay of Pigs, where they had totally screwed up. They said, if I had done my job, there wouldn't have been the Bay of Pigs.

A "reporter" who supposedly worked for the *Miami Herald* kept putting notes under my door saying it was urgent for him to speak with me. When I finally spoke with him, he warned me that I was "marked for death," that I should drop the suit against Marcos.

I was walking with Monica in her stroller when a red car headed straight towards me. I jumped and pushed the stroller out of the way but was hit myself. As I rolled on the ground, I got the license plate number. I was badly bruised and had severe abdominal pains. I picked up Monica, abandoned the stroller, and limped home. I called the police and reported the hit-and-run, then went to Mt. Sinai Hospital in an ambulance. I lost my five-month-old unborn son.

On August 13, 1963, the judges agreed that Marcos had to leave. On August 16th, I raced to the airport in time to see an emaciated Marcos being led up the ramp to the plane in handcuffs. Carrying Monica, weeping, I ran down the runway, but was tackled by federal marshal and led away in handcuffs.

Within a week after Marcos' extradition, the rug was pulled out from under me. I lost everything—my home, car, Monica's trust, everything.

Walters' tenth floor law office burst into flames and was destroyed. The fire, confined to the office, was discovered early in the morning and had been burning for several hours. All records were lost.

Monica was without her father. I was broke. I was homeless.

7

Once again, I contacted Frank Sturgis and the gentlemen of Op 40. I had a child to support and they offered a means to that end. I moved in with a couple I was friendly with. He was a CIA contract employee who was in Op 40. The people who visited them at their house—Sturgis, Orlando Bosch, Pedro Diaz Lanz, and other hard core enemies of Fidel Castro— delighted in my hatred of Bobby Kennedy and my anger at the U.S. government's actions against Marcos. The same actions had deprived me of what I believed to be my rights as the mother of Marcos' child could well have been behind what I felt was the deliberate murder of my unborn baby. My coworkers saw in my anger that I was ready to do anything.

I ran guns again. I delivered briefcases filled, most likely, with money or drugs. I didn't ask. I stole boats and occasionally sank them and their cargos of contraband guns when I felt I needed to say "fuck you" to all sides. Everyone trusted me for the most violent acts; they also realized I was out of control. My new nickname was *Alemana Peligrosa*, the dangerous German woman.

They all knew my history as Fidel's lover (or victim), my forced childbirth (or abortion), and my anger towards (or love for) him. Despite or because of how they viewed me, they accepted me. I found loving support, a degree of understanding, and approval. I made them my extended family. Their thoughts, feelings, and attitude mattered more than the reality of my situation.

That was why I kept trying to please Brigade members and the others who had sent me to murder the man I loved. That was why I felt lost without their companionship. Gradually, over time, I lied to myself until I came to believe that they were the only people who would ever accept me.

On April 17, 1961, the Miami Cubans and Brigade 2506 sent 1,400 men to Zapata Swamp, expecting full air cover, extra ammunition, and complete Navy support. The full story has been written elsewhere many times. What is relevant is that the United States allowed the Bay of Pigs fiasco to take place, failing to provide the military force needed for success. There were many villains in the story, but in South Florida intelligence and paramilitary circles, John Kennedy became the focal point of blame for the failure.

From the time I rejoined Operation 40 after Marcos' deportation, all I heard was "We're going to get Kennedy," "Let's get Kennedy."

A lot of books have been written about the assassination of Kennedy. By the time Congress reopened the investigation into the assassination in 1978, there was no question that several people were involved.

At that time, I testified to information concerning the events that follow before the House of Representatives Select Committee on Assassinations. It is all a matter of public record.

The men of the 2506th Brigade and their supporters were delusional. Everyone they knew hated Fidel. They were living in exile in a community made up primarily of wealthy Batista supporters who had always been a minority elite. They were friendly with American business leaders who were actually organized crime figures—Mafiosi—another minority in the United States. They kept themselves isolated, training for battle and living together in areas where they spoke only Spanish.

Why learn fluent English when you are going to return home to where you won't need it? Why read American newspapers when they do not feature what is taking place in Cuba? Why consider the majority of Cubans who had suffered under Batista when you either had lived your life in isolation from them, were elitist and thought they would do what you said, or did not want to face the harshness of your parents' actions towards them? Given such social, political, and intellectual isolation from what was actually taking place, they truly thought that the people who had welcomed Castro with joyous faces two years earlier would suddenly welcome their return. They believed that men and women who were beginning to get an education and decent health care would want to take back rulers who had denied them both. They thought that people who had suffered from crop losses they had caused would somehow forgive them.

When the Bay of Pigs mission failed, they did not see their own foolishness, Instead, they blamed Jack Kennedy.

In recent years, several facts have become known. First, according to one of his lawyers, Jimmy Hoffa was actively involved in planning a hit against the president. Hoffa, the Teamsters leader who had been targeted for jail by Bob Kennedy, wanted to destroy the Attorney General. However, he, along with his friends within the Mafia, all felt that if they killed Bobby, there would still be efforts to get them. Jack Kennedy would simply appoint a successor who shared his brother's obsession. However, if they killed the President, two things would happen. First, Bobby would be demoralized and ineffectual for a period of time, which did occur. Second, Lyndon Johnson would enter the White House, and Johnson hated Bob Kennedy. He would sweep Kennedy loyalists out of the Justice Department and replace them with men who were more concerned with civil rights than with organized crime.

Carlos Marcello, whose organized crime family was actively involved with the casino gambling in Havana, hated the Kennedys. He had been illegally deported to Guatemala by Bob Kennedy. He also felt betrayed by the failure to oust Castro and restore the casinos to his men. He, too, wanted Jack Kennedy dead.

In November, 1962, Kennedy made a stop in Miami in order to return the flag of the 2506th Brigade. He made an appearance in the stadium, commiserating with the Cubans because he had fully expected the flag to fly over a "free Havana" when the Bay of Pigs succeeded. Just prior to his arrival date, Sturgis, Bosch, and their friends talked half seriously of shooting up the stadium in protest. They did not make the effort, though Kennedy was soundly booed by the Cubans in exile, a fact that was downplayed in the news.

Talk of assassination became increasingly serious. I thought they were all nuts. I thought that they would never see a free Cuba because the Cubans on the island did not share their vision. Castro might have been somewhat ineffective in his leadership, he may have been thwarted by the blockade and trade embargo against him, but everyone knew he genuinely cared about people who had been disenfranchised by the elite of society. I figured that no matter what we did, nothing was going to happen.

After hearing Kennedy's speech at the stadium, several of the leaders said, "That fucker's going to die because he let us [the Bay of Pigs invaders] die."

129

MARITA

We made another raid on an armory for weapons.

As I testified before the House assassinations committee in mid-November 1963, Operation 40 members gathered at the home of Orlando Bosch to sit on the front porch, drink Cuban coffee, and talk. Sturgis and Bosch brought up Dallas, Texas, and proceeded to spread a street map of Dallas on a glass coffee table. They were making travel plans. I liked the idea of getting away from the Everglades, the safe house, Miami. I didn't care about their exact plans, so I left the porch and wandered through Bosch's garden, picking oranges to eat.

I heard Sturgis say, "She goes. We can use her."

I was one of the best shots in Op 40, so if there was a possibility of violence, I was taken along. I was also the sexiest assassin they had, so I was used as a decoy, as in the armory raids. And I was the best person they had to handle boats. If a maneuver required navigation, I was a natural. I don't say this to brag. These facts were probably the only reasons I hadn't died in a training "accident."

I didn't ask questions. I was always ready to go, always wearing the black regulation jumpsuit almost everyone in Op 40 wore so we could instantly engage in night covert actions. I always kept a bag packed with the equipment I would need for either land or sea activities.

However, unlike earlier days, I now had Monica. Willy May lived in Homestead, Florida, and would take care of her, though I resented being away from her. It was one thing to know she was safe. It was another to have the emotional drain of being separated from my baby. I asked how long we'd be and was told, "It's just up the coast a ways."

Having made certan Monica would be okay in Willy May's home, I went to sit in one of the two cars that would be used for what I assumed was to be a "feather merchant" (gun running) trip. I was tired and bored; I fell asleep while weapons and

130

other supplies were being loaded into the back. I was awakened by the slamming shut of the trunk. Then everyone piled in around me. Sturgis was there, along with Pedro Diaz Lanz and Bosch.

The second car transported a man earlier introduced to me as "Ozzie." He had been to the Everglades several times with us. He was an American, a skinny guy, relatively out of shape. He couldn't carry or lift anything, or participate in any of the training exercises. He gave me the creeps; he had a serious attitude problem towards everyone.

Sturgis told me to shut up when I complained about Ozzie. "He'll serve his purpose."

I was reasonably comfortable in the car, a four-door navy blue sedan with big tail fins and four sets of license plates we could change at will. It was the standard car for these runs.

Treating me like "one of the boys," Sturgis issued his orders: "No broads, no booze, no [telephone] calls, keep everything low key." It was what he always said.

If anything was different about this trip besides the destination and the presence of Ozzie, who had never gone on a run before, it was the number of weapons in the trunk. As usual, the men carried whatever handguns they preferred. I carried my .38 short revolver with smooth hammer and a .25 automatic. In the trunk were handguns and automatics, machine guns and rifles, .38s, .45s, tripods, scopes, and shotguns, with ammunition for everything. We also had C-4 explosives and camping gear.

The weaponry we carried would only be used for a murderous mission. The rifles were excellent assassination tools for fairly long range. The handguns were powerful for close combat, and included some that could shoot through the crankcase of a car. The shotguns were perfect for tense situations, both close and at a distance, because the pellets covered a wider area than

131

a single bullet. This assured a hit even when the shooter was nervous and a little shaky. In close, they would destroy a man.

The C-4 explosive could be used for a diversion or to bring down a highway overpass. It would make an excellent car bomb or serve any other purpose where a compact, easily concealed and detonated, moldable, powerful weapon of death was desirable.

Sturgis also carried personal disguises. He had a clerical collar with him so he could look like a priest. He had the clothing to look like a bum; if he chose to use it, he wouldn't shave so he would have at least a day's stubble of whiskers. He had expensive clothes to make himself look like an Italian businessman. The trouble was that he wasn't particularly articulate.

The men did all the driving on what proved to be a two day, nonstop trip. I slept most of the time. The men slept and then took amphetamines to stay awake.

I awakened to see the Texas route signs overhead. We were on the outskirts of Dallas where I heard Bosch tell Sturgis how to find a certain motel. He was excited, pumped with adrenaline, as he said, "Man, this is the BIG ONE!"

"Hey, what the hell is so special about this job?" I asked.

"Never mind," said Sturgis. "Just sit tight and follow orders."

Then, joking, I said, "No, really. Who do we have to kill?"

There was a moment of stunned silence. I didn't know if I had touched a nerve or what. I really didn't care. Nothing about that world was real, and whatever I was told to do in the group I would probably do. After a moment, Sturgis angrily said, "Shut up, Lorenz." So I shut up.

We parked at the motel. Sturgis registered us as a hunting party. That way, if anyone saw our weapons, no one would be upset. The handguns could be concealed. The C-4 was not noticeable. The rest of the weapons were good for hunting. After all, stalking a deer, stalking a bear, or stalking a man were all the same.

We took two adjoining motel rooms, each with two double beds. The men staked out their territory, then began taking showers. Pedro tossed me a spare pillow. The gear I was carrying could serve as my mattress for all they cared. I was going to sleep on the floor between the two beds.

There was more than disdain being shown to me. Yes, there was hatred and jealousy. I had failed to kill Castro, yet I was one of the best shots and did better in training than most of the men. They needed me, but only if I would do exactly what they said. Making me sleep on the floor was another effort to break me.

An agent I'll call Gerry came over. He had been in the other car along with two Cuban brothers named Novis.

Of the group I worked with Gerry was the most likeable. He hated the Novis brothers. He told Sturgis and the others in my room to leave me alone. I suggested he and I tell the others to screw it and go back to Miami. Neither of us meant anything by it—we were just tired and didn't like being kept in the dark about what our mission was to be.

Sturgis repeated the instructions: "No outside contact, no phone calls, no broads, no booze." Then he went out to unload the trunks, bringing everything inside where it could be hidden under the beds while we slept.

I was shocked by the quantity of weapons. Having slept through the loading, I hadn't seen our arsenal. We could also become anyone. We had an immense variety of disguises to prove we were who we chose.

The weapons and disguises would allow us to do anything from assassination to taking over a building. Yet no one would

133

tell me. Gerry knew no more than I did. I was expected to do what they wanted.

If they wanted to treat me like a girl, I'd act like one. "Hey, Bosch," I said, seriously. "I need some Kotex. Who's going out for some?"

No one answered. In those days talking about your menstrual cycle was upsetting to most men, especially the Cubans. The idea that a man would have to go to a store to buy a feminine hygiene product filled them with horror. And none of them had the brains to realize that I knew I was a woman, knew my time of month, and would pack whatever I needed.

"Okay," I said, cheerfully. "I'll just bleed all over everything." One guy laughed, realizing I was just trying to upset them. The rest looked sick.

Somebody opened the door to the adjoining room where Gerry and the others were staying. Ozzie was sitting on the bed, and again I wondered why he was there. I had never seen him shoot, though I figured that if he was good for anything, it must be that.

Later that night, some time after midnight, Eduardo, who I identified during congressional testimony on the assassination of John Kennedy as E. Howard Hunt, stopped by. It was November 21, 1963. He gave Sturgis an envelope filled with cash which Sturgis counted and approved. He was there for about an hour, then left. He has always claimed that he was home in Washington at the time.

I was mad at everybody, at their macho bullshit. I knew we were there to kill somebody. We had to be. The money was an advance payment for something. We each got a cut. I didn't count mine.

It must have been two o'clock in the morning or a little later when there was another knock at the door.

The man at the door was a mob guy, typical of those hanging around Havana in 1959, so typical he looked almost familiar.

Well dressed, heavy set, middle-aged, of medium build, wearing a hat, he had the look of a disreputable businessman.

"Hey, what's that goddamn broad doing here?" he asked noisily.

For once Sturgis came to rescue my "honor." He backed the guy out the door, then began swearing at him. But the mob guy must have been more important than Sturgis in whatever the hell we were there to do. He finally lashed, out "You fat son-of-a-bitch. Who the hell do you think you're talking to?"

Sturgis got nervous. I could hear him fighting for control, trying to quiet the situation. "Shhh. It's okay. She's with us. She's okay."

"Look," said the mob guy, "I don't do business with broads."

"I said she's one of us," Sturgis snapped back. "She knows Fidel personally."

I didn't know what Fidel had to do with any of this. Was he going to mention I screwed up the mission to kill him?

With the exception of the birth of Monica nothing had gone right since I had gotten involved with Marcos. Now I was in Dallas in some stinking motel room where we were armed to the teeth for a mission they weren't telling me about. And just outside the door, some mob punk was telling Sturgis that he didn't care what skills I had or who I knew. "She's still a broad."

That was it. I was pissed and disgusted. I committed enough crimes for the CIA that, if I had been a civilian, they'd toss me in jail and let me rot. I could handle a boat better than any of the men. I could handle weapons at least as well as they could, and I had a hell of a lot more stamina than their boy soldiers. I could be a woman where it mattered. I had proven I could be a soldier where it mattered. And now I was being called a broad by some fat mob guy who had probably ass-kissed other mob

135

guys to become whatever the hell he was. I'd had it with this operation. It had never felt right to me. Besides that, I missed Monica.

"Screw this mission," I told them. "I'm going home."

I packed my personal gear. The mob guy was smug. He had shown his power. In my mind, he was a good reason to walk away.

Sturgis tried to talk me out of leaving. I didn't know how much cash I had with me, but I knew it would be more than enough to get home. Whatever they stuck in those envelopes was always more than enough. I intended to fly to Miami.

I wasn't alone in disagreeing with how things were happening. Gerry also walked out on them.

Later I saw the wise guy's picture on television, then in newspaper and magazine photographs. There was no mistaking him. He had been the lowlife I thought; it had earned him the right to manage night clubs in Dallas. As an assassin, his record as a hit man for organized crime dated back to 1939. He had been an FBI informant in Dallas since 1959. His name was Jack Ruby, the shooter who would soon kill the man I knew as Ozzie—Lee Harvey Oswald.

I took a cab to the airport on November 21, 1963. Crews were putting "Welcome, Kennedy" signs on poles along the way. I paid little attention to them. The president had been to Miami and I was not impressed then. So what if he was coming to Dallas? My interest was getting back to Monica.

As soon as I hit Miami I drove to Willy May Taylor's house in Homestead where Monica was being cared for. The home was an odd contrast to the rest of my life. Willy May, my nanny when I was living with Marcos, was a nobody to world leaders. She was a woman who had lived her life in poverty, raising six children in a home with limited plumbing and an outside toilet.

Her children, however, were better loved, nurtured, and cared for than those of most of the leaders trying to decide the fates of nations. Together we enjoyed the luxury of the Marcos era, though she knew it would never be hers and was fully aware of my position. I spent many wonderful, happy days with her that otherwise would have been very lonely. On one occasion, she even saved Marcos' ass from his enemies. She was my dear friend and companion, my Black Mama. She will always be in my heart.

Willy May was worried when she heard about Dallas. She knew nothing more than I did, though she understood the significance of the men and the guns. She had worked for Marcos, and unlike me, she was not naive. She listened to the conversations and met his men. She understood instinctively that whatever was taking place in Dallas was more meaningful than I let myself understand. "Lord have mercy, child, you best be making fast tracks," she told me, encouraging me to leave Miami to visit my mother in Fort Lee, New Jersey. "You be in some bad company now."

Willy May was right. She suggested I spend the night in her home and begin making arrangements to take Monica from Miami to Newark Airport. She fed us all a dinner of ham hocks and grits, then put me to bed on a mattress with three of her children.

It was November 22, 1963, and as we approached Newark, the copilot's voice came over the loudspeaker:

"Ladies and gentlemen, we regret to inform you that there may be some delay in landing because the President of the United States has been shot in Dallas, and the airport may be needed for official departures."

I screamed. Then I began sobbing quietly, uncontrollably.

I could prove nothing. Frank Sturgis admitted he was in Dallas and taunted reporters by refusing to say he was not a

137

shooter. Ozzie was arrested, then murdered by Jack Ruby who in turn died awaiting trial. There were photographs of all of us together, photos taken in the Everglades. Alex Rorke took them to document our CIA activities—covert operations, even a group shot of Op 40. This action was bitterly resented by some brigade members. The prints I had were turned over to government investigators. Alex mysteriously vanished from the earth. On his death as well, I cannot prove my lingering suspicions.

As I have testified, I believe we were all part of an assassination team, heavily armed, well-trained. Ozzie was probably part decoy, part throwaway. Undoubtedly, he was a shooter, as has long been assumed. However, the clandestine, illegal activities taking place on home soil would shock even the most sophisticated and cynical American citizens.

This hit was a big day even in the life of Operation 40. The head of state who had been targeted happened to be in the United States of America. The CIA had miscalculated their ability to control the wrath of a band of Cubans in Miami.

For a few it was business as usual.

III

JUNGLE
IN
VENEZUELA

1

I talked with the FBI. My report was dutifully noted in the files. But my report would have compromised information about covert CIA action and was buried in top secret paperwork. Even if Op 40 had been no more involved with the shooting than I had been, the statements would have revealed that the government was illegally arming and training an army to deliberately violate international treaties. The truth about Frank Sturgis, Orlando Bosch, and the rest of us had to be kept from the public. The fact that we might have revealed the full story of the assassination meant nothing.

Robert Kennedy, once the most aggressive of all law enforcement officers dealing with organized crime and organized labor, was shattered by his brother's assassination. His staff said he felt his own mortality. He became better known for challenging the elements through white water rafting without a life preserver than for trying to find the truth about his brother's death.

Actor Peter Lawford, a Kennedy brother-in-law, admitted to private family meetings where no one believed that Ozzie acted alone. They saw other factions, though their belief was that the murder was financed by a pair of wealthy, Dallas-based businessmen. But no one did anything about their suppositions.

J. Edgar Hoover did not want the investigation to go farther than the Warren Commission would take it. He had warning messages in his files that were received months before the assassination, yet these had not been passed on. People sympathetic to the director said it was because he did not take the reports seriously, an error of judgment, nothing more. Others, who found the reports after they were opened to the public, felt that his hatred was so profound, he did nothing to intervene.

The Warren Commission itself was tainted by the pasts of some of its participants. Michigan Congressman Gerald Ford was a key member of the Commission. Many of his constituents belonged to the powerful Teamsters Union which had contributed to his election campaign. It was doubtful he would look too closely at people who helped keep him in office.

Others with dirty little secrets related to affairs of government would not be revealed to the American people for another thirty years. What was important right then was that no one make waves in the confusion, ignorance, apathy, or greed of the nation's power figures. In the end, nobody in power positions really wanted the American public knowing the truth. Ozzie was the scapegoat for everyone's sins.

I had no idea where to go or what to do. My mother had her own life and work. I had no intention of returning to the Everglades. I had to protect Monica. I had always been told that no one involved with covert operations should have a child. There was no time for motherhood, for any personal life. Life was too cheap, the demands too great.

Out of nowhere, in 1964 two Immigration and Naturalization Service agents, came to tell me I had to leave the country. Although I had a U.S. passport, they claimed I wasn't a citizen.

I was the child of a Nazi father, was German. I was told I was an embarrassment to the United States and to get out. I assumed it was the result of my vehemently opposing Bobby Kennedy's request to drop the paternity suit against Marcos, thereby holding up his extradition.

I was destitute. The only thing of value I had left was Monica. I decided to take her and go to Venezuela. I was going to march to the prison in Caracas where Marcos was awaiting trial and demand to see him. I was feeling brave. I had nothing to lose. I was being incredibly stupid to give in to their demands so easily. But if my country had decided it didn't want me, so be it.

Both Marcos and the Venezuelan government leaders were pragmatists. Marcos had loved me in Florida. He wanted a child, and he was delighted to have a daughter, even though he was expecting a son. But that was Florida where he was comfortable. He had me, his bodyguards, his financial causes, bribes, and an occasional visit from his wife. When he left Florida, he was wrenched from that world with all the callousness he had shown when he ruled Venezuela. Now he had to endure prison life, a hardship no worse than being sentenced to five years in a hotellike atmosphere because of the deals he had made for himself. Yet with that prison sentence, and with his plans for exile in Spain when he was free were new priorities and new concerns. I was not among them.

The United States government was not eager for me to precipitate a needless international incident. I was enough of a problem because of my connections with the Kennedy assassination and with Fidel. The Venzuelan officials were alerted that I was coming.

A fellow passenger on my Viasa Airlines flight gave me his business card and said to call him when I got into difficulty,

143

because I *would* get into trouble. He was a businessman. He supplied the Venezuelan military with boots.

It was easy for officials to identify me because I had to present my passport. My passport was for Marita Lorenz and Monica Mercedes Pérez Jiménez. Officials immediately knew who I was.

I never was allowed to get my luggage when the plane landed. Agents from *Servicio Información Fuercas Armadas*, the Venezuelan military intelligence office, arrested me as soon as we disembarked onto the ramp. Five men, two in plain clothes and three uniformed officers, surrounded us. I refused to set Monica down. Two of the men gently grasped my arms, guiding me to the room where I would be questioned. The rest of the officers gathered my diaper bag and other possessions. One of the men had handcuffs out, though I said that they were not necessary. No one tried to hurt me, though it was obvious to me they would use whatever force was necessary.

I was taken into a private room where a tough looking female officer was waiting. My papers were checked. I asked them what I had done wrong.

Marcos was in jail. The baby and I were of no threat to anyone. I had some fear that the men might be Marcos' enemies with plans to hurt us in order to get at him. Yet Marcos retained a strong following in the military, and the officers who were there weren't hostile. They identified themselves and told me I had been apprehended for questioning. They were very polite.

The guards searched my luggage for guns and other contraband. They asked me why I was in Venezuela, and I told them that I was there to see the father of my child.

"Who is that?" they asked, smirking.

"Your former president," I told them.

Then I learned why the woman was there. I was going to be strip searched. A strip search is the most demeaning aspect of

144

being in jail for both men and women. It is intended to demoralize and degrade. Just as upsetting is the reason it is done: Prisoners routinely hide drugs and weapons in all their body cavities. For everyone's safety it is considered necessary. I told them absolutely not, and eventually persuaded them to back off.

There was no stopping the determined guards. Two days before my arrival, an arms cache had been found in the capital city. No one was certain which revolutionary group had stockpiled the weapons, though they were believed to have ties to Fidel. My history with the Cubans made me a prime suspect.

The officers were still not convinced I was there only to see Marcos, not to lead an army of terrorists. They agreed to take me to Marcos in what proved to be a place that looked like an ancient castle located at the foot of the Avila mountains just outside Caracas' center.

We traveled in a small caravan of olive green military and unmarked cars. I felt no fear. I tried to joke with them. I asked if they would let me go through the city to see the landmark buildings that Marcos had built. They did not react. They just kept driving.

The prison was a four- or five-story structure that looked as though it had been built centuries earlier. I met the captain who was in charge of the facility, El Moro. I realized I was under arrest when they walked me down the hall and placed me in a bare cell approximately seven feet by ten feet. There was a vent but no windows, a cement bunk, a sink for water, and a hole in the floor that served as a toilet. The guards shut and locked the door to make me more "comfortable." The only possessions they let me have were my empty diaper bag and a roll of Lifesavers. How ironic. Monica and I were clearly not welcome guests of the new Venezuelan government.

The cell had a barred door through which you could see a

courtyard surrounded by cells on all four sides. There was one sad palm tree and a fountain in the middle. It might have been a Ramada Inn with a Spanish motif built by a sadistic architect.

The captain came by to explain the situation to me. Very politely, he told me that I was not to bother the guards for anything because they were not sympathetic to my circumstance. Each man had been handpicked to guard the prison where Marcos was being kept. Each had come from a family that had suffered in one way or another at the hands of the Pérez Jiménez government. In many cases they were the sole surviving member of a family murdered by his staff. Others came from families who had lost their property or otherwise endured hardships as a result of his regime.

The captain took me to an interrogation room. No one believed that an American woman with a child would be foolish enough to come to Venezuela to see their thieving, imprisoned former dictator. The only possibility was I was undercover.

I explained to the captain about losing the trust that Marcos had established for the care of my daughter, about being hit by the car and losing Marcos' unborn son. I explained that I had been expelled from the United States, was without a country. Since I had always loved Latin American culture, and with Monica's father being here, I had hoped to be able to relocate to Venezuela. I thanked him for his protection and for putting me up. At the moment, I said, I just want to see Marcos.

The captain realized that I was the person who had held up the extradition by filing the paternity suit. I could not tell if he disliked me for it. However, he would not tell me exactly where Marcos was in the prison, other than that he was near.

Neither of us was certain what to do. I had wanted to go to a hotel when I arrived, put on makeup, and then see Marcos. The castle was just a place to stay during the visit, like a Venezuelan guest house. The reality was quite different. My

BEAUTIFUL MAMA
SURROUNDED BY
PHILIP, JOE, AND
VALERIE.
I'M ON HER LAP.

↙ MAMA

ME

ME   PAPA   MAMA

BEFORE THE WAR

ME   7 YEARS OLD
    AFTER THE RAPE -
    REFUSING TO SMILE

17 YEARS OLD -
JUST BEFORE F.C.

PAPA'S SHIP, THE MS BERLIN

PAPA AND FIDEL TOASTING ON BOARD THE BERLIN

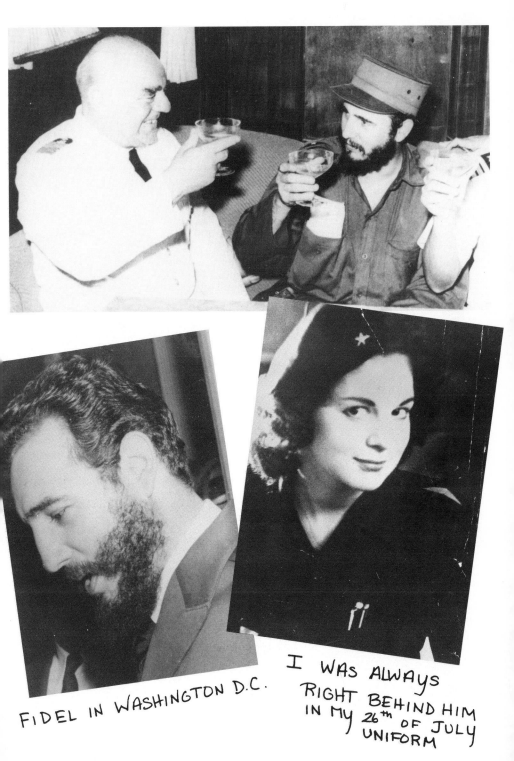

FIDEL IN WASHINGTON D.C.

I WAS ALWAYS RIGHT BEHIND HIM IN MY 26th OF JULY UNIFORM

AGE 5
LITTLE MONICA MERCEDES PÉREZ JIMÉNEZ

GENERAL MARCOS
PÉREZ JIMÉNEZ,
THE FORMER
PRESIDENT OF
VENEZUELA

1963
BABY MONICA
AND I WAIT
WHILE THE
PATERNITY SUIT
AGAINST MARCOS
IS BEING
REVEIWED

1977 - HOLDING A
PHOTO OF MARCOS
AT A NYC
PRESS CONFERENCE

xpräsident wird ausgeliefert

Die Vereinigten Staaten haben gestern entschieden, daß der im Jahr 1958 gestürzte und dann in die USA geflüchtete frühere venezolanische Präsident Jiminez an Venezuela ausgeliefert wird. Dort erwartet ihn u. a. ein Verfahren wegen angeblicher Veruntreuung von 13 Millionen Dollar Regierungsgeldern.

YANOMANI
WOMEN
EMERGE FROM
A "SHAPONA"
A TRADITIONAL
CIRCULAR
HOUSE

TAKEN BY F.B.I. AGENT -
R. JAFFEE

FRANK NELSON AND FRANK STURGI

CHARLIE "THE BLADE" TOURINE
"UNCLE CHARLIE" TO ME

ME SURROUNDED
BY CLIPPINGS
OF CASTRO

CUBAN REFUGEE PRISONERS - DELTA II IMMIGRATION DETENTION
BARRACKS

GUARDING 600
REFUGEE ORPHAN
CHILDREN

(VERY SAD)

CUBAN REFUGEE
"RELOCATION
   CAMP"
FORT CHAFFEE, AR.

MONICA

MARK

MONICA MERCEDES
My BEAUTIFUL DAUGHTER,
IS COMPETING FOR
MISS FITNESS U.S.A.

captors had limited options in dealing with me, something I did not realize. I was asked if I wanted to talk with the American embassy, but I did not, reminding him I had been told to leave. An ambassador, I thought, wouldn't do as much for me as I might be able to do for myself.

Finally they took me back to the cell. My understanding was that I was not under arrest. I was just being detained, albeit under lock and key. I was given the impression that if I made trouble, I would be treated like the other prisoners. When a prisoner grabbed the bars of his cell in protest, a guard would use his baton to smash his fingers. Brutality was routine.

One guard walked with me to the cell. Another carried Monica, who looked adorable in her lederhosen—leather pants with daisies, red suspenders, and white booties. She was the delight of almost everyone who saw her, despite looking amazingly like Marcos. But when I was put in the cell, Monica was not placed inside with me. Before I could grab her, the door was closed and locked. As I watched in horror, the guard carried her off in the direction of the interrogation office.

I shouted at the guard to give me back my baby. I was fired with anger, but he was calm, explaining that she would be fine. When the guard kept walking, I panicked. I was certain that Monica was going to be taken away from me or killed. Her death would be a way to show disdain for her father, to hurt him and me.

I shouted to the captain to return my baby. My voice grew shrill. I began screaming louder and louder. The other prisoners joined in, shouting at him to return Monica. He ignored us all.

I knew the only person who might be able to help me was myself. I must appeal to the captain's fatherly instincts. Marcos was supposed to be "near," whatever that meant. I had not seen him. I had not heard his voice. But if he was near, I was going to make certain he heard me. I called his name shouting as

147

loud as I could. The prisoners got silent when they heard Marcos' name. Again and again I called to him, telling him as best I could where I was in the prison. I was determined to make such a scene that something would happen, something would change. Anything.

Then I heard a voice, little more than a whisper yet loud enough for me to hear when I wasn't shouting. "Shut up!" he said in Spanish, sternly though softly. "Shut up!" He did not identify himself, though I knew immediately.

"Marcos," I said. "Where are you?"

"To your right," he replied.

I looked up at the vent. That was how he communicated.

The cell block was designed to give maximum security to normal detention. I was in a standard cell with the barred door through which I could see what was taking place. Next to me was one of the high security cells with a solid door and a slot for passing through food. Although I didn't know for certain if Marcos was in there, since the venting could have also led to other parts of the jail, I suspected there was a direct link. Marcos, so far as I could tell, was locked in the sealed cell next to mine.

I tried to find something on which to stand, but there was nothing. I had kicked off my high heels, but even putting them back on would not help. I was just too short, the cell's furnishings too spartan for me to be able to climb closer to the "intercom."

"Why is you here?" asked Marcos.

I told Marcos how I had been attacked by the hit and run driver, how our unborn son had been lost.

Marcos cursed, then explained that it was dangerous for me to be in Venezuela at that time. His trial had yet to begin.

"What should I do?" I asked.

"Go to Spain," he told me. "Wait for me." That was where he would eventually go into exile. I would be safe there.

He wanted to know why I had brought the baby.

"Because I had to see you."

Suddenly one of the guards shouted at us to be quiet. I don't think he knew what was happening, other than that there was unauthorized conversation. Angry, I shouted back, cursing him. Then I heard him coming towards my cell. I knew I'd pushed my luck.

I sat back on the bunk, not wanting the guard to know I had been talking with Marcos. I listened to the guard's boots, to the cleats that were attached and were clicking noisily as he walked rapidly along the walk. The sound recalled one I had heard when I was in Drangstedt, the SS children's home in Germany and in the concentration camp at Belsen.

Instantly my mind raced back in time. I remembered the doctors and the guards. I remembered the terror and the punishment. I remembered my growing horror as I realized that I was "impure," that other children were suffering even more in the same camp.

I tried to remind myself that Belsen was a memory, not the present moment in Venezuela. Yet the Nazi brutality and disregard for life could be imitated elsewhere. Hadn't Marcos had a reputation for allowing his enemies to be tortured? Monica and I were directly linked with a man against whom others wanted vengeance. Monica could be enduring far worse than anything I experienced. Monica could be . . .

"Monica!" I screamed. "Monica!"

I cursed the guards who separated us. I cursed Marcos. I cursed the man who sounded so much like one of the Nazi soldiers. I was out of control. Again the prisoners took up the cry of "Give her the baby!"

"I want my baby!" I screamed. "Don't touch my baby!"

I began pacing back and forth like a wild beast who suddenly finds herself caged. I have never been claustrophobic, but I do not handle forced confinement well. I moved to the side where Marcos could hear me best, calling his name, demanding his help, as futile as that was. Then I moved to the door and cursed the guard, demanding he return Monica to me. Back and forth I went. Back and forth. I refused to give up, to be silent.

"Give the kid to the mother!" the other prisoners shouted, no longer reacting to Marcos.

I began kicking at the bars, trying to shake them. I was near hysterics as I shouted my name and said that I had a baby with the general. I told the prisoners, "You're my witnesses. We can't let anything happen to my daughter. She's just a baby."

The prisoners took up the cry. "Let her go! Let her go! Give the kid to her mother."

Nobody among the guards would answer me. Tears began rolling down my cheeks. The tears turned to wracking sobs. I was hyperventilating, my body heaving as I gasped for air, unable to gain any sort of emotional control.

I was afraid they would give Monica away. She was half Venezuelan and her father was a hated, deposed dictator. I thought she would disappear the way my son with Fidel had. She would be raised without ever knowing her biological parents. I felt doomed and terribly drained.

My mouth grew dry, my head began to hurt. I experienced flashing lights inside my head, followed by blinding pain. It was the onset of a migraine headache, something I could count on during a troubled menstrual cycle.

The pain became intense, the sole focus of my thoughts. I wanted to pound my head against the concrete, as though I could smash open the skull and let the pain fall out.

I lurched to the sink for some water, but the faucet did not work. I had not eaten. I felt a surge of nausea.

Suddenly there was silence. The silence was broken by a baby's cry. It was Monica. She was still close at hand, yet she was not being brought to me. I could hear her, though I could not see her, touch her, assure myself she was safe.

I dropped to the floor and rolled myself into a ball, trying to find a position that might ease the pain. I felt as though I was undergoing the tortures of Hell.

It was hot, humid, my head was exploding, and I heard my baby's cry. Yet I could not scream any more. The pain was too great.

The crying continued briefly, and I went crazy again.

Suddenly the captain appeared, holding Monica. She had a big bottle of milk, a cookie in her hand, and a smile spread across her face. She looked at me, a half-wild woman curled on the floor, and happily said, "Mama!"

Silently I thanked God,.

The captain was apologetic. He said, "I am a father. Don't worry." Then he told me that the crying had come only because he had been careless and she had fallen off a chair. She was fine, though her diaper had needed to be changed. He said that he had his assistant do the dirty work. Monica was just beginning to be potty-trained and she had not yet learned how to alert a stranger to her needs.

The captain was frustrated by everything that was taking place. He couldn't be the warden in charge of the men and a babysitter at the same time. He knew enough about my background not to trust my motives. Yet, as a mother with a toddler, I was sympathetic. No one wanted to hurt Monica or separate her from me for very long.

I looked at Monica and the captain and started crying, this time from relief. The cell door was unlocked so she could be given to me. I was told that food and fruit juice were being prepared for her.

I was given my suitcase which was in disarray. The security force was taking no chances. They had gone through everything, looking for weapons, microfilm, or anything else that might reveal a secret agenda.

The cell was made more comfortable for us. Blankets and pillows were brought in. The sink was repaired, though the water had been turned off long enough so that when it was turned back on, it came through a filthy brown color. I was brought a bucket of fresh water for drinking.

After dark the captain returned to the cell. Orders had been given to incarcerate us. There was to be more questioning in the morning. However because of Monica the incarceration would be in a more comfortable confined area.

Apparently the captain had been busy making arrangements with government officials who were involved. I carried Monica out of the cell, along the courtyard, and past the other prisoners. Marcos, if he was still there, was in one of the solitary cells with a sealed door. I did not see or hear him, though the other prisoners said goodbye, calling me "Little Mommy" and wishing us good luck.

Suddenly I was in the midst of flashing cameras. The press had been alerted to my presence. They wanted interviews. They wanted pictures. The next morning the papers were full of front-page stories about Marcos' "common–law wife."

It was midnight when Monica and I were taken to the hotel. There were two cars this time, and we drove rapidly through Caracas, then up to the Avila mountains. I was given a guided tour of the area by the captain, and a combination of uniformed and plain-clothes guards. I was familiar with the folk music and the literature, and I began quoting the books I had read. The captain was impressed, telling me that the General had taught me well.

We entered the hotel where I was to be held from the back steps. I was given a suite with a balcony offering a spectacular view of the city of Caracas and the mountain community below. The air was sweet with tropical sea breezes. I felt a rush of freedom when I stepped out on it, even knowing there were guards in the adjoining suite. There was a baby bed for Monica. Everything was quite comfortable. The food brought to the room was well prepared, but fear of its being laced with drugs or poison never left me.

As I prepared for sleep, I could hear music rising from the valley below, and I could smell the bougainvillea in the night air. A dozen roses were brought to the bedroom, along with a card welcoming me to the Andes. There was no name attached, though I suspected that the Captain had sent them as a way of apologizing for the emotional hell I had undergone when separated from Monica.

At seven A.M. the next morning, there was a knock on my door. I had had only a few hours' sleep at best.

The officers informed me that it was time for questioning at the palace.

This time I was seated at a large table. A couple of dozen officers were present, apparently the military and government high command. They wanted to know about me, about my life with Marcos, about my work with the Cubans. I was photographed and fingerprinted, as was Monica. Men were brought into the room to look at me, though who they were or what their identification might have meant, I never knew.

Apparently my past was better known than I had realized. I had forgotten that I still carried my dual membership cards— one for the 26th of July Movement and the other for the anti-Castro organization. In their minds, only a spy would carry

153

both. If I was Castro's lover, why wasn't I living in Cuba? And what was the connection between my background and the Marcos/Fidel feud?

I tried to explain that I wasn't with Fidel anymore, that I was involved with Marcos. They knew I had a child with Fidel. With Marcos in jail, in their minds it made sense for me to be in Cuba. I had children by both men; Fidel was the one better able to care for me.

Certain information about Marcos came out during the interrogation that I had not known previously, much of which I have never been able to verify. Despite his extortion of American companies doing business in Venezuela, he seems to have been one of the CIA's South American darlings. Before losing power, he was given the Legion of Merit award by President Eisenhower.

Most of the interrogation, however, focused on Fidel. For nine days we sat at the large mahogany table, Monica running around, climbing on the laps of the men. She was being potty trained, but there was no easy access to a toilet, so she was in diapers. Every hour or so one of the military men would get a surprise package. Then I would take her to the bathroom to change the diaper, one or more of the men escorting me.

The reasoning of the military leaders seemed to be that, if I were willing to come to Venezuela in pursuit of Marcos in jail because he was the father of my daughter, what would I do for my other child? Would I be willing to work as a terrorist or spy for Fidel? Would I be willing to try to foment revolution?

I kept trying to explain my position, but my position was complex. I had one child by the dictator of Cuba. I had another child by their former dictator. Were there any other dictators with whom I was involved?

There were also legal questions. Monica's first language was Spanish. She was half Venezuelan. And she looked exactly like

Marcos. She had rights in their country, and because I was her mother, I also had rights. Since I made clear that I would not be going back to the United States, they did not know what to do with us.

Over that nine day period of the interrogation, I was being investigated independently as well. The men determined that I was not the person who had helped plan or plant a hidden arms cache. They still thought it might have been someone working for Fidel, and I agreed that was possible.

"We don't want anything to do with Fidel," they told me.

"So tell him that," I said.

"Would you do it?" they asked me, apparently thinking I might act as a liaison with Cuba.

"No!" I shouted. "No! No!" I repeated again that I had nothing to do with Fidel any more. I wasn't going back to Cuba. "Didn't you ever have a girlfriend and then you were through with her?"

They asked me what I thought they should do with me. I told them they could treat me like a tourist. I wanted to see the country. I wanted to hear their music. Or they could make me Venezuelan. My money was gone. I had nothing.

It was explained to me that Marcos' wife and children were in Peru and that he would be jailed for twenty years. I said that I would wait, which caused one of them to burst into laughter. He said, "You'll only wait until you find another dictator."

I laughed, too. With my history, he was probably right.

Finally I was presented with a paper on SIFA letterhead. It was a statement swearing that I had not brought any people or weapons for destabilizing the country. I signed it, after which both Monica and I were photographed for their records. Then I was told that I was free to go.

But go where? What should I do? I said that I knew Marcos

155

owned several homes there. If they told me where they were, I would stay in one of them.

The men just laughed at me. They said that Marcos had robbed the government. His homes had been confiscated. He had no more property there.

"So which one of you has a spare bedroom?" I asked the men.

They enjoyed the humor. I was given my passport, an extended visa allowing me to stay in Venezuela permanently, and hugs all around. I explained that I only had a couple hundred dollars so they would have to decide what to do with me. Then I was returned to the hotel where there were more roses waiting.

The military leaders arranged to escort me around the city. I took Monica because I still did not trust them enough to leave her with a sitter at the hotel. We went to an elegant dinner with the captain and four other officers.

The captain told me that I could become a citizen if I wanted. I agreed. I asked them to begin the paperwork the next day, though they warned me that putting the Pérez Jiménez name on the application could cause me trouble. I had to agree with their reasoning, so I didn't go ahead with it.

For two days I did nothing but rest, read, and enjoy Caracas. Then, at four A.M., I was awakened by a knock at the door. I was told that I had an hour to get ready to go.

I had no thought of danger. We had left the interrogation amicably. I thought they knew my plight, liked Monica, would not consider hurting either of us. I assumed that I would be taken to one of Marcos' confiscated houses to live. I hoped it would not be the one he maintained on the island of Margarita. That had been the love den where he kept his prostitutes, where he went when he wanted to provide himself and his buddies with his decadent form of rest and recreation. He established these little love dens everywhere he lived. It was a side of his personality I didn't want to be reminded of.

I was looking forward to my new life. The early hour was probably to avoid the reporters who had been so curious when I arrived.

An air force officer transported me to a military air field. I was placed in a twin-engine, four-seater Cessna. We were the only plane at the runway. On the ground were men armed with automatic weapons. The captain said I was going sightseeing, to see Venezuela.

The sun rose as we flew across the country. The sights were magnificent. There were ore fields in the velvet green mountains, the colors as rich and dark as blood.

Our destination was Ciudad Bolívar, the last civilized stop on the Rio Orinoco. From the air, as we approached the military landing field, everything looked beautiful but isolated. There were tiny houses on the banks of the river, though it appeared there might be only a handful of people.

When we landed, I was taken to a house that looked like a small version of a Swiss chalet. There was a tiled courtyard and a garden. The house was beautifully maintained as a private hotel by an elderly couple. It was to be my home, a location in isolation, peaceful, with plenty of food and clean water.

The elderly woman worked needlepoint. The man tended the vegetable garden. There were old paintings on the walls. My bedroom was clean and well appointed. It was like being in a country inn without a telephone or television. The only entertainment was from a record player on which they played recorded harp music.

The men who brought me there left. They said they would be back "soon." In Latin America the word "soon" could mean anywhere from three weeks to three years.

I was told to call the caretakers Adela and José. They were

obviously trusted by the government. They were my servants and my jailers. I never went to a store, never saw them go anywhere for supplies, yet I always was given anything I needed. There was fresh fruit. There were toys for "Moniquita," who was two and a half by now and speaking full Spanish sentences.

There were beautiful birds, a pet dog, and even a small pet monkey. No one wanted to kill me. No one wanted to interrogate me. No one wanted me to play war. I had no thought of tomorrow. I was at peace.

Over time I learned that the area had perhaps 200 residents in all. I was the only "visitor." The only access, other than by plane, was a dirt road leading back towards civilization. Everything beyond this small area was unexplored. We were the last location carved from the jungle.

My room had shutters instead of screens or storm windows. I left them open so I could view the foliage, and because I hated the feeling of being confined if I kept them closed. There was a fan for cooling which added to our comfort. I had no responsibilities except caring for Monica. The couple talked with me endlessly, but always about "safe" subjects such as Venezuelan history. There were no newspapers, no current books.

One morning, after three weeks, I heard the gate open. It was the pilot who had brought me there. He had made nasty remarks about Marcos. I had feared him, feared that we might be hurt, but such fears no longer existed. The weeks had been an unusual interlude, the most relaxing weeks of my life.

I walked into the courtyard to meet with the pilot. "So you'll be right back?" I said, facetiously. I didn't like the man, and it was obvious that he didn't like Marcos. However, I saw no reason not to believe him when he said that he was taking me sightseeing again.

I was told to pack for a flight which I thought would be to Caracas, where Marcos owned houses. However, when we took off in the plane, we flew in a different direction. The pilot made light of it. The copilot said nothing, as before.

We flew for hours, along the Orinoco, past the Jimmy Angel falls, and on, South East, the land ranging from brown and scrub to the Andes mountains to jungle that looked like a green carpet.

"Do you want to see the Indians of Venezuela?" he asked.

"Not particularly," I said.

Then he began flying like a daredevil—going straight up in the air, banking sharply, skimming mountain tops. Monica was crying, terrified.

Sometimes there would be a patch of brown in the midst of the green foliage. The pilot explained that, wherever I saw the brown, there was an Indian settlement.

"Do you want to see me piss off the Indians?" the pilot asked. Without waiting for my reply, he did a steep dive onto the brown clearing, going low to the treetops, frightening the natives and making them scatter.

I told him to stop, but he didn't. He said that the Indians did not like white people, that the inhabitants of one of the settlements had eaten the anthropologist son of Nelson Rockefeller—though I knew full well that had happened a continent away. He said that if I smiled at them to be friendly, they would take that as a sign of insecurity and kill me. He said that they liked to eat white women, to take heads for ritual display.

As the pilot went low over one village, I could see the natives running naked below us. Several of them had blow guns which were used for hunting that fired darts tipped with poison.

When the pilot descended again, the natives aimed their dart guns at the plane. There were two thumping sounds as two of the darts struck the belly of the plane. Then the pilot pulled up, opening the window and waving at the terrified people.

"We're gods," he told me. "They think the plane is a bird from heaven."

The pilot took out a map and began studying it with the copilot. The two began arguing over where they were, though they were not lost from what I could tell. We were approaching Brazil, a fact they pointed out to me.

The pilot began looking closely at his fuel gauge, as though worried about how much fuel was left. I was concerned with the time, wanted to head back to Caracas before it was dark. I had the feeling that everything they did was meant to scare me, that everything happening was well planned.

Suddenly an overgrown airfield appeared below us. It was near a mining camp that had been abandoned. I could see nothing, no major jungle clearing. We were along the Orinoco River. Tall grass—six feet in height I realized when I eventually left the plane—looked as though it could absorb the shock of a rough landing.

I clutched Monica as he said, "Hang on!" Monica was crying. Buffeted all about, the plane bumped down hard through the grass. Grass broke through parts of the cockpit. I felt as though the plane might pitch forward, or that the propeller would snap. When the pilot opened the door, he had to cut away the vegetation from the propeller and wings.

I was concerned. How were we going to get out of there?

2

Amazed at the big bird from God, naked Yanomano Indians—children, men, and women—ran towards us. The males chanted, their spears and sticks pointed at us. I didn't want to leave the plane, but the pilot said it would show too much fear to hide inside. The heat and humidity were overwhelming.

Monica and I were the objects of attention while the pilot tended to the plane. As if to test the runway, he turned the plane around and gunned it back over the grass tracks where we had landed. I grabbed Monica and ran towards the plane. He pitched my bag out the door and started to lift off. I screamed, ran, fell, yelled, "NO, NO, don't leave me here!" I looked up, waved frantically until the engine sound was totally gone.

All that could be heard was the chatter of the Indians and birds, my sobbing, and my curses. Monica cried because I cried, and a small naked boy patted her. I stared at the Indians and they stared back at me. They looked menacing and vicious.

The children started amusing Monica. The men grabbed my bag, and I grabbed it back. An old woman took off Monica's

161

lederhosen and examined them; she sewed them into a water bladder. I sat looking up at the sky until a red-orange burning sunset almost blinded me.

I walked into their clearing. There were thatched huts, men in hammocks, women kneeling, tending fires or weaving. They touched me, stared, gestured. I sat on the ground, leaned against a tree. It was getting dark. I was scared absolutely shitless.

That night was hell. Holding Monica, covered with bugs, exhausted, my head on my bag, I cried myself to sleep. I figured that if I wasn't clubbed, raped, or beheaded by morning, I'd live to await the plane, which I expected to return at some point or other.

At dawn all the women went in a line on a path into the jungle. I walked to the river bank and went to the bathroom in the brown water without removing my jeans. Something moved and slithered past my leg. The men, swinging in their hammocks, laughed at me as I freaked out and ran from the river.

I was terribly hungry and thirsty. Pointing a finger to my mouth, I was given water in a shelllike cup and a bunch of bananas. I took out my pocket knife and carved Monica's full name on a tree. They looked and admired my "art." I smiled. So it went, little by little.

Every day I carved an "X" into the tree.

Monica, by the third day, was stark naked. Only her long black hair and slightly lighter skin distinguished her from the others. (Her father was part Indian.)

I did a lot of watching. What bothered me most was the ear, nose, and lip piercing. I had a thing against physical mutilation. I worried about them doing their "art" on Monica.

I watched the men return from their daily hunt. Using spears and blow guns, they brought down tapier, monkey, fish, wild pig, anteaters, birds (including a sort of turkey). They cut the skin, pulled it off, bled the animal, gutted it, and put it over a smoldering fire. Sometimes they put a whole monkey, hair and all, over or in a fire pit and singed off the hair. The smell made me gag, but I ate the meat.

We ate Brazil nuts, mushrooms, palm hearts, eggs, casaba, melon, mangoes, sometimes honey, and a lot of things I didn't recognize. The most terrible thing to eat raw were fat, round little white slugs plucked from palm leaves. I gagged. The Indians loved them. When I put one or two on a stick and held it over the fire, they took the stick away.

I was laughed at when I washed in the river. Then my soap ran out. My fingernails were broken and dirty. I put my hair in braids. I looked into the sky for the plane that never came. My face got sunburned. I was pestered, day and night, by insects and covered with bites.

Almost every afternoon a heavy hard sheet of rain broke the monotony of humidity and oppressive heat and gave temporary relief from the insects. As soon as the rain stopped, the jungle steamed, and more bugs than ever returned.

I started to try to spear fish. Even the children and Monica were better than I. (The fathers made the children little hunting bows, spears, and arrows.)

They gave me leaves to rub on my scrapes, scratches and bites. A fierce looking, painted and scarred Indian gave me a bed of leaves, reeds and straw. I gave him my powder compact in gratitude. He was so happy with the mirror that all the other Indians tried to take it from him.

Snakes were everywhere. I constantly feared for myself and Monica. Even the Yanomamo feared them. Once I saw four Indians drag a huge, twenty-foot-plus boa into the camp, alive. The kids tried to ride it until they were shooed away. I grabbed Monica and ran.

The males had two or three wives, loving all equally. There

163

was absolutely no jealousy among the women. Each male could have all the wives he could support by hunting, fishing, building thatched-roof huts, and weaving hammocks. If he failed to provide these things, the other Indians would pound their chests and fight for his woman. They would spit on and insult each other, until a new man won her.

After about six lines of five notches in the tree, I started to become sick. I couldn't control my bowels or keep food down. I shook and felt weak. I doubled over with severe stomach pains. I was burning one minute, freezing the next. I began to hallucinate snakes, sacrifices, black tunnels.

I had contracted malaria. I was sure I was dying.

As I lay in a semi-conscious state, an elderly Indian woman forced water down my throat and made me chew leaves. What seemed like weeks later, I awoke from my "death" to a floating world. I was very thin, very weak. I was put into a hammock. Kashishi, the elderly woman, became my Indian mother. She kept me chewing the bitter leaves. They made me vomit and gag, but made the pain go away. I felt light, "spaced out."

I began to pick up Yanomamo words and phrases. "Hekurra," I learned, was the spirit who protected me. I never said the word "Yakirri" (I'm scared) again!

I stopped crying, stopped looking to the blank skies for the plane that never came. I was ready to shed the past, the drifting nightmares of my "civilized" world.

I cut my hair, threw away my soiled blouse and shoes, held hands with the women. I no longer thought of the people as barbaric or uncivilized. Suddenly, everything they did daily made sense to me. In fact, everything had its place and timing—birth, eating, hunting, building, firemaking, teaching and loving the adorable children, telling of spirits and gods, telling happy and sad tales. I tried to grasp their culture, their language. I felt reincarnated. Spanish, German, and English became part of my past life.

Months went by. Monica was over three years old. We talked together in the Yanomamo language.

When I was carving her a doll, I cut my finger badly. The children brought me a bunch of leaves and pressed them down on the deep wound, then covered it with a thin tree vine. Within hours, the wound had stopped bleeding and closed.

I so envied the Indians. They were organized, simple and perfect as long as the outside world left them alone. I wanted to free my thoughts from the persistent past, to look not to the sky but to the earth.

I started to make a garden and to build my own hut. I wandered with a spear through the jungle. There were amazing varieties of orchids and amazing sounds. I found my God in the natural world around me, every living creature, plant, cloud. I felt as though I was, with the Yanomamo, an original member of the family of man, as close to God as anyone could get.

I had a native admirer, Katcho, who speared and brought me half-dead wriggling fish. The soles of his feet were wrinkled, white and cracked from standing in the river for hours, patiently targeting his prey. Once he brought me three piranha on a spear—red-bellied, fierce-looking bastards. He slapped them until dead and showed me their razor-sharp jaws. The Yanomamo didn't like them; they would divert a school of "ranhas" downriver with a white toxin, then go fishing at another end of the river.

My admirer was a strapping golden-red-brown solid un-scarred pure male with splayed-toed flat feet, hair cut in bangs and stained red with berry juice. He put his nose to my face (a sign of affection) and clicked his tongue and mouth (a sign of pleasure). He brought me fruits and berries, and followed me with his eyes.

One day when I went into the jungle for berries and wood, I found that he was stalking me. I played hide and seek, but he was much wilier at it than I. I worried about losing the path. As I crouched alongside the trail, he found me and knelt down beside me. I knew when his hands touched my breasts and he gently coaxed me down that this was it!

I looked at his eyes, his square face, even mouth, and I didn't resist. He put his blow gun, spear, and poison arrows down on the ground, untied his loincloth and unbuttoned my dirty jeans. Moaning, with ecstasy in his face, he rubbed himself all over me, then exposed his erect huge penis proudly and penetrated me, moaning, rolling, in a sexual frenzy that became mutual. Pure sex, unashamed, physical, erotic. The twigs and branches cut my back, and the ants and bugs swarmed everywhere, but we kept going. He regained his erection again and again. We tried various positions and discovered every inch of one another's body. This pure body of pure man made me sexually wilder than I have ever been.

It started to rain. Our bodies were wet and exhausted. Katcho got up, picked up his weapons, and put on his loincloth. Over and over again he repeated a word I didn't know. Returning to camp, I felt guilty, wondered if I could have gotten myself pregnant. I slithered into my hut and hammock and held Monica ever so close. Katcho eyed me and went to the elder chief to buy me as his wife.

Our "marriage" worked this way: after dawn, when I gathered firewood, he followed me, and we'd tackle each other. He already had another hut, wife, and child, but there was no jealousy.

According to my rough reckoning by the moon, almost eight months had gone by. One morning when I was washing in the river, I heard a droning overhead. The sound sent dissonant signals to my now tranquil mind. I shook my head and wet hair in angry contempt for my old thoughts. I hurried nowhere, and stood defiant against the sun and sky as the engine of this invading plane drowned out the songs of morning birds and disrupted the peace of my camp and the routine of my morning chores.

I felt invaded. Anger rose in me. I lifted my spear and, with all my strength and a rebellious cry, flung it at the sun. All my family of Indians, except Katchu, ran to the overgrown clearing to see the big spirit bird come down from the sky.

Katchu stood in front of me. He held my arm and guided me out of the water. Without emotion or will to move, I sat on the river bank.

Four uniformed military men, one carrying a Red Cross bag, walked hurriedly through the camp. I sat on the ground, holding my wet knees. No words would come out, no language, no emotion. Katchu, blow gun in hand, stood defensively next to me. As the officers approached me, I clung to Katchu's leg. Their eyes showed disbelief, pure horror at the sight of me.

They talked rapidly, trying to coax me to go with them. Monica, naked, clung to me. The Yanomamo got in a line, stamping and shuffling their feet, lifting sticks, spears, blow guns, and emitting a shrill shriek from their mouths. The women and children retreated to the huts and hammocks.

"We're here to take you to the U.S. at the request of your mother," said the man with the Red Cross bag.

3

I was admitted to the Miami hospital with 103° fever. I was diagnosed as having malaria, dysentery, and miscellaneous skin wounds. Monica had been bitten by something on the nose and had a high fever, nearly fatal, for three days. We were hospitalized for a week.

Later I learned that my exile had been either coordinated with the CIA or the CIA had kept track of where I went. My exile was not the decision of Marcos' enemies, at least not theirs alone. I had challenged the attorney general when I filed the paternity suit and tried to keep Marcos in Florida. I had failed to kill Fidel. I new too much about people who had gone to Dallas the day before the assassination of the president. I could not be controlled as part of Operation 40. I was traveling into Latin America where that could affect various negotiations and anticommunist activity against Cuba and elsewhere. I knew too much, said too much, and did too much. I did not fear their power. No one dared murder me because of my mother's power in the National Security Agency. That didn't mean they couldn't leave me someplace where I might not have the skills to live.

Mother learned all this and with the help of Irwin Charles Karden, backtracked through reports and statements until she found me. She was furious at what had been done, furious that it had been done to her daughter. She was the one who arranged for our rescue.

I went to live in her apartment in New York.

IV

FUN
IN
NEW YORK

1

My "Uncle Charlie" lived at 40 Central Park South. His apartment was magnificent. He had seen a picture of an apartment in *House Beautiful* magazine while he was in jail. It so impressed him that he tore out the page, kept it until his release, then hired someone to exactly duplicate it.

This was Charlie "the Blade" Tourine, who must have gotten his nickname from the way he treated his enemies. I had known him since I was a child when Papa docked his ship in New York. Uncle Charlie worked for men like Eddie, who controlled the mostly Irish longshoremen at Pier Ninety-Seven on West Fifty-Seventh Street.

Eddie was the pier boss where Papa docked his ship. Although he and his brothers were like tall, powerful tanks, comfortable using physical violence in order to control their rough longshoremen, Papa treated them as associates. They came on board the ship when it docked, mingling with customs officials and others who had legitimate business there.

Papa was a master at the game of diplomacy. The chef fixed the best food. There was the finest whiskey; if a man had a favorite, a bottle accompanied him as he left. People and situations were handled with subtlety and tact.

Eddie was the largest of eight brothers, all of whom were powerful. I once saw Eddie, almost seven feet tall, become angry with a stevedore who had knifed another dock worker. Eddie picked up the assailant and tossed him into the water between the boat and the pilings.

I was special to these men. I was the Captain's daughter, "The Little Captain." The men were rough. The hooks they carried were for grappling with massive containers as well as for fights. But they were gentle with me, kind, seemingly my friends.

Uncle Charlie liked having Monica and me hang out in his apartment. He adored Monica. He changed a room into a nursery, even though we were not living there, and took us to buy toys at F.A.O. Schwartz, just down the street. He cooked great Sicilian meals for us. All he asked was that I guard his apartment and the maid when he flew to the islands. He entrusted me with his alarm security code and the $2 million dollars in cash he had stashed in a shoe box. He was a gambler.

I hung out with Charlie almost daily. One day I showed him a magazine story I thought would interest him. To my amazement, he told me he couldn't read. I told Charlie that I would teach him to read, but he was uncomfortable with the idea. His excuse was that that was how he was planning to stay out of jail. If he couldn't read, there was no way he could know what the law was. Ignorance of the law would keep him a free man. I pointed out that ignorance of the law was no defense, and it obviously hadn't helped him in the past. Finally, I convinced him that he could learn to read without telling anyone.

I began teaching Charlie the alphabet. Then I made him copy words and simple sentences, such as, "My name is Charlie Tourine." We worked on this day after day. We bought children's books for Monica at F.A.O. Schwarz. He read her books, and passed on to her the ones he liked. Both were learning together, though he moved faster. I tried cutting out articles for him from the day's papers. His interests were primarily gambling, organized crimes, and himself. After a couple of months he was able to read what was being written about himself in the newspapers. "I like to read what these bad bastards have to say about me," he said.

Charlie also read to me over the telephone when I couldn't be with him and he was trying to learn something new. I even taught him how to read the knobs of the stereo he owned; he had always worked it by trial and error.

I began dating a man I'll call Andy. He was extremely handsome and he made a lot of money—literally. I was impressed by his looks and amused by his sense of humor. Charlie warned him, "You touch her, you're dead." He had no intention of letting anyone fool around with me, even if I wanted it.

Andy earned his money laundering counterfeit money. He took me on one of his trips to drop off a package, and when I realized that the bills he was selling looked pretty good, I told him to give me some. The World's Fair was being held in New York that year (1964), and I figured I could use the money there. Andy had nothing to lose so he threw me a couple of piles, and I had a few thousand dollars in play money to spend.

Passing the money was a game to me. Andy told me it was made in someone's basement in Brooklyn. You had to look closely to know it was no good. He told me to pass it in places where the lighting was low, such as in bars, or where the cashiers were under pressure. Long lines of people waiting to get on popular rides or other attractions were good places to get change. No one had the time to make more than a cursory study of each large bill. I was able to pass a couple of thousand

175

dollars a day without getting caught. It was a challenge to see if I could get away with it.

The story of the funny money hit the papers a couple of months later, though my involvement never was mentioned. Charlie was outraged. In his mind, anyone who passed the money was working against the country he loved. You could kill someone "for business," but dirty money was a crime. He was even angrier when he discovered I was one of the people passing it, that I still had some left. He made me give it to him so he could rip it up and flush it down the toilet.

"You're a lady. You're not a member of the Mafia. What do you want to be, a bad guy?" he yelled at me.

"Yeah," I told him. "I want to be bad."

I was feeling better. My health was improving. My weight was increasing. I was getting bored and just itching to see what I could get away with.

"You need a job," said Charlie. His voice sounded like someone's Puritanical father. He may have spent his life in crime, but "The Little Captain" was going to be an honest woman.

"I'll get a job," I said, being cocky. "How about a hit lady for the mob? Or maybe I could be a Godmother. Can you make me a Godmother for the mob, Charlie?"

Charlie was serious. I wasn't. Finally we settled on a compromise. Charlie sent Monica and me to Paradise Island in the Bahamas. We were given a suite for a month, Uncle Charlie arranging for everything I needed. It was where Charlie sent the big time gambling junkets, the ones exclusively comprised of high rollers who would spend thousands of dollars a day.

Charlie's associates escorted me to the shows at the casinos. They were all gentlemen, and they all treated me with respect. It was a wonderful vacation, though it was on an island and brought back more memories of Cuba than I wanted to remember.

When I returned to New York, Charles had arranged for me to go to work at the Statler Hilton Hotel where, ironically, I had stayed with Fidel when we were there. They needed a receptionist, and my language skills were helpful. However, I didn't like the job. They had one of those switchboards that had a series of plugs and jacks for making connections. I was shown how to use it, but I couldn't get it right. I connected the wrong parties at times, and disconnected others before they were through with their conversations.

2

I started to go out with a Cuban named Umberto. We got married and set up house in 1965. I knew him as a handsome man, a great dresser, someone who treated me wonderfully on dates. There was no affair this time. I just married him.

One day Umberto's briefcase popped open. The contents fell on the floor: burglar tools, two pistols, lots of cash.

I left Umberto a note saying I wasn't ready for marriage and asking for a divorce. Before I left, I took two packages of money, about $5000.

About two months later, I found a pawn ticket he had given me. Out of curiosity, I presented the ticket. Immediately I was surrounded by detectives. It was for a stolen Leica camera, one of the most expensive available at the time. Umberto, it turned out, was wanted by the N.Y.P.D.

I was attracted to and started dating J.J., one of the arresting detectives, who was recently divorced.

I still had the $5000 from Umberto's briefcase. The N.Y.P.D., as well as FBI and Secret Service agents, were still hunting him. I used some of the money to enroll in a language school and in criminal justice courses, and carried hundred dollar bills in my jeans pocket for spending money. After school, I met J.J. for coffee.

When I met him one day, five months afterward, in a German restaurant on East 84th Street near my apartment, his radio crackled. They had located Umberto. J.J. left and called me later. "Holy Hell's a-blazing," he said, "your ex was into counterfeit."

"Oops," I said, feeling the hundreds I carried in my jean pocket.

That night, I felt guilty as hell, and more furious than ever at Umberto. I had even paid the tip for J.J.'s and my hamburgers in the German restaurant.

The good girl in me said "give the bills up and say where you got them." The daring, adventurous bad girl in me said, "Go for broke, and pass them." I blew some and kept some to send to people I didn't like. To clear my conscience, I "fessed up" to Uncle Charlie. He had a complete fit. He tore up the bills I showed him and flushed them down his toilet.

"Don't you ever dare touch that stuff again, do you hear me?" he screamed. He stormed to his closet door and banged it with his fist. "Look, there's two million fucking dollars in a shoe box on top. You need money? You always got it! Take it! You're a good mother. You don't want to end up in the can. You gotta hang up the guns and forget the past, just forget it!"

Charlie made me think. I was playing a dangerous game. I could lose Monica. She was my life and my joy.

Charlie called my mother. "Mama," he said, "Marita's too angry about the past, '59, '60, '61, '62, '63, '64, '65, '66. She's playing cops and robbers. She has no direction. How's about you and me sending her home to Germany?"

Before I left for Germany, I met with J.J., who informed me

that Umberto was doing time in Sing Sing for a jewelry store stickup with assault on a police officer.

I needed Umberto's signature for the final annulment decree. J.J. drove me up to Ossining. I got the signature by promising to send Umberto packages, which I never did. Before I left, he said he had been a CIA Alpha 66 Brigade member in Miami, but had a falling out.

I said, "You know, Umberto, you really are a piece of shit! You run from Cuba because you're a bum or Fidel kicked you out. You come to the U.S., work for the CIA, but it's too dirty for you. You come to New York and rob innocent hard-working people and think you're above the law."

I stormed out of Sing Sing totally disgusted with myself. A guard said to me, "What's a beautiful young girl like you doing with a low punk like that?"

You're right, sir, absolutely!

3

Monica and I went to Germany to visit my father, who was dying of cancer. We stayed with my Uncle Fritz and Aunt Lotte in the house where Papa was born, in the village of Bad Münster am Stein in the Rhine Valley. We went to the hospital every day, then worked in the garden and explored the vineyards and orchards. My aunt and uncle taught me to be an excellent cook. They were wonderful, seeing me through a heartbreaking experience.

Papa died on July 14, 1966.

After that, I thought of settling in Germany to work and raise Monica. But I returned to the U.S. to live with my mother on East Eighty-sixth Street. I put Monica in a private school and began taking classes in medical school. I often wrote to Marcos in jail, to keep the memory of him alive for Monica.

Marcos was released in 1968. The papers stated he relocated to Madrid, named the hotel where he was living, and the men who followed him.

I set up a tape recorder with telephone coil pickup and called Marcos. He said he was overjoyed that I called. The minute the phone rang, he claimed, he knew it was me. Yes, he'd gotten all my letters and pictures and saw how beautiful his daughter was, how much she looked like him. He said he was terribly upset about the invalidated trust and agreed to make it good. I should come over and talk to him.

I said, "Oh did you hear that Bobby Kennedy was killed?" He replied, "Yes, it's good. He deserved it."

"Jesus, Marcos, how can you say that??"

"Very easy."

"Were you behind it? Because of the extradition?"

Marcos said, "No more! I talk to you when you come over." He changed the subject, asking if I'd like to live in Madrid with Monica. I said yes.

Monica talked to her *papi*. He said he loved her dearly and told her never to forget who her *papi* was, that we would all be together soon.

I played the tape back for my mother. When the part about Bobby Kennedy came up, my mother turned white and was horrified. "My God," she cried, "he brazenly talks like that on an open international line about a candidate for President of the United States who was murdered?" I never heard the end of it. She was convinced that Marcos had the means, money, and motive to accomplish the dirty deed.

Years later, I heard that Marcos was questioned by investigators who suspected his involvement in Bobby Kennedy's assassination.

Like others, on that cold overcast day, I had gotten up at five A.M. and stood in line at St. Patrick's Cathedral to pay my respects for the second Kennedy who died so violently. I knelt before and touched his flag-draped casket. Although I'm not religious, I said, "God, Bobby, I'm sorry I gave you a hard time back in '63 in Miami. Sleep now, and I hope to God that Marcos had nothing to do with you being dead here now!"

I went home, disturbed, thinking how Jimmy Hoffa and Marcos were both under the gun in Bobby's obession to rid the U.S. of organized crime and set an example to future dictators not to settle in the U.S. Various newspapers, books, and records estimated that Marcos was worth in excess of $700 million, and still receiving oil revenues and kickbacks from Venezuela— enough money to have anybody eliminated, for sure.

I flew to Madrid the following week and checked into the Castellana International Hotel. In the morning I went to the dining room for breakfast. Before I got back to the room to call Marcos and tell him to send Pedro Estrada to pick me up, I suddenly became dizzy and weak. I couldn't get my breath. Every bone, muscle, and joint in my body ached. I barely made it to my room, where I flopped belly down on the bed. I was sure somebody had put something in my food or coffee.

I passed out and awoke to someone shaking me and a voice with a British-sounding accent asking if I was all right and should he get a doctor. He said he was walking past my room, saw the door was open, and heard me moaning so he looked in. He said his name was Frank. He was a businessman from Australia. I told him no hospital, just help me get the first plane out of Madrid to the U.S. I mumbled out Mama's number in New York, which he called. I was convinced the CIA was trying to stop me from seeing Marcos.

For two days I languished, weak and in pain, with Frank taking care of me. He promised to get me on a plane as soon as I could walk. On the third day I could stand without falling. He helped me pay the bill and got a cab to the airport.

My mother was waiting for me at Kennedy Airport with an ambulance. At New York Doctors Hospital, my physician diagnosed my condition as the result of an "unknown toxin." I was in the hospital for a week, then returned home.

I got the message.

183

4

Around this time Ed and I became close friends. Ed had experienced terrible personal problems and was sympathetic to me. He was an insurance salesman who had grown up in Brooklyn. Some of his associates were the sons of men involved with the mob. Those associates bought insurance from him. Ed inherited race horses, owned thirty-six trotters, and was involved with a number of organized crime figures—the "Kosher Nostra," he called them—connected with the racing industry.

Big money was available to Ed. He spent lavishly on me, including buying me a four and one-half carat diamond ring.

Ed had been through a period of personal tragedy. His daughter died of a brain tumor the same month that both his mother and father died. His marriage fell apart; he was separated. He told my mother that he wanted to marry me when the divorce was finalized. The ring served as proof of his intentions.

I couldn't marry Ed. I couldn't marry anyone right then. I might have gone to Marcos had he asked me because he was Monica's father. But that wasn't an option. Ed insisted I keep the ring anyway.

One of the people Ed paid to do things for him was Louis, the manager of our apartment building on the upper east side. Louis seemed a rather straight guy, nice, handsome. He had a job that required his being part handyman, part diplomat, part businessman. The advantage was that he was given a rent-free apartment, a definite plus in New York. Despite the fact that Louis worked hard, he always seemed above it all, acting more like owner than manager.

When I wanted some cabinets built in Monica's room, I tipped Louis and asked him for help, which he gave me. It was the universal situation in New York, tipping the manager to get something done. Nothing was out of the order except the way he held himself.

I learned the truth about Louis the same day my medical school class watched an autopsy. Part of our medical training was to observe what happens when the coroner has to rule on cause of death. The technique is cold, impersonal, and extremely upsetting the first time you see it done. Police officers have been known to faint, so I suppose I can consider myself stronger for only getting a little nauseated.

I planned to forget the experience as quickly as possible. I planned to go home, change out of my white uniform, start dinner, take Monica for a walk while it was getting ready, then eat, and go party. The trouble was, the moment I entered my apartment building, Louis met me and asked me to come into his office. Inside I found two FBI special agents, Uncle Al and John.

"I want you to meet my friends," said Louis, his attitude rather cocky.

"I never believed you were just a superintendent," I said to Louis, who just laughed at me. "Who are you, really?"

The men were revealing their FBI identities because Monica was friendly with the children of a tenant who had a large suite on a floor above us. The tenant was a woman, a single parent, either the daughter or stepdaughter of one of the top mobsters in the United States. Our children used to run around the halls together. I thought the woman was quite nice. However, Louis said that in addition to being a good mom, she had a clothesline hung in her apartment for drying counterfeit money after dipping them in tea to age them.

I was asked to make friends with the woman. I was to provide the Feds with reports so they could build their case. She was involved with manufacturing to some degree, and if convicted, she was going to do jail time despite having the children.

"Come on. You're going to make me a snitch? I'm not a snitch."

"Marita, we've read your file," they told me.

"Look," I said, "I don't want to be a snitch. I just want to go to school, be a good mommy, and fool around. If you've read my dossier, then you know I've lost everything. I don't want to go back into that life."

I didn't get involved in that investigation, but they put together a case without me. Her apartment was raided, funny money was found in large quantities, and she went to jail. There were cops everywhere on the floor.

It was all rather uncomfortable. I still had a small bundle that I hadn't shown Charlie. It was my little joke to use it in the mob connected clubs, crumbling it as though it had been in circulation for a while. It was my idea of having a little fun.

The FBI agents kept coming back to me in Louis' office, trying to get me to work with them. They knew my history, but they did not understand how I had been used and abused. I didn't want to repeat the past. I didn't want to risk being hurt.

The men kept pushing me. I became quite friendly with Louis. He was longtime FBI, his specialty being undercover assignments that often lasted several years. He had worked with

Uncle Al on other cases, including one on a Canadian nuclear power plant believed to be infiltrated by Russian spies. However, he told me very little about his past.

When Ed failed to divorce his wife when he said he would, I became interested in learning what Louis was made of. One night when my mother was out, I invited Louis to our apartment. We talked for a while, and then I seduced him.

During this time when I was seeing both Ed and Louis, I got pregnant. I was using a diaphragm as a contraceptive. I was one of those women for whom the diaphragm had seemed a hundred percent effective, so I never worried about having another baby. The pregnancy came about because of a sheepdog I had at the time.

Snuffy was one of those animals who was big, friendly, adorable, and into everything. One day he went into the bathroom when my mother was home but I was away. He managed to open the medicine cabinet and get the container that held my diaphragm. He knocked it around just enough to leave a hole in it. Unfortunately you had to look closely to see the damage. When my mother found it, everything looked normal. She placed it back in its container and returned it to the cabinet shelf without telling me.

I was so angry with the dog, I gave Snuffy to a friend who loved dogs and had a garden. He became a companion and a guard for his owner's store.

So I got pregnant because of a dog. Ed thought he was the father. I did not tell him that Louis was.

I realized that I wanted the child. Monica talked constantly of having a brother. I knew that, no matter how difficult, the chance to love a second boy or girl would be wonderful.

Louis was stunned but happy when I told him. His world was one where a child would be at risk. He had a new undercover assignment coming up and a family was not anticipated. He never suggested I get rid of the baby. He was just stunned.

Ed was also delighted with the prospect of becoming a father again. He wanted me to marry him. However, he was not yet divorced.

Ed also paid for the education I was getting at the time. I was attending the Eastern School For Physicians on Sixteenth Street in Manhattan. He was proud of me. One morning I arrived for classes as usual, only to be thanked for paying off the tuition. The cost was approximately $5,000 per year, and like most of their students, I was paying by installment. Ed's surprise gift was further proof of his caring.

I began experiencing nausea during the pregnancy. This compounded my problems. Eventually it became a situation comedy. I had been dating a police officer in addition to my relationships with Ed and Louis. I was also still making certain that Marcos was truly finished with our relationship. As a result, there were days, when I was home from school, when I was on the telephone trying to locate Marcos in Spain. Louis was building a nursery for the baby. Ed was bringing me gourmet meals so I could keep up my strength. And downstairs in the lobby, the police inspector I was dating was waiting for me. I met the inspector when I had applied to work for the New York City Police Department.

Ed's horses were at the Meadowlands, Roosevelt Raceway, and Yonkers. Sometimes we flew together to Kentucky or other states to buy new horses including one for my new son. We traveled by private plane, having a great time.

The FBI agents were interested in me. They wanted me to work for them. They also genuinely seemed to care about what I was doing. The information in my file indicated that I had intelligence experience. It also indicated that I had had serious problems in the past.

"What are you doing?" the agents asked me.

"What do you think I'm doing?" I replied. "I'm baking a baby."

"It's not good to bring a child into the world without a father," they told me.

"A lot of things aren't good," I told them. I knew they wanted something from me.

"What do you really want from me?" I asked.

They suggested I marry Louis in order to give my child its natural father's name.

The situation was actually more complex and less pious than that. They had an undercover assignment for which they felt they needed two people they could trust. Louis was a special agent. I had the background and training so I could take care of myself. Together we would make a perfect team.

There were some "minor" details to take care of, as was usually the case with that type of law enforcement. I had to give birth before I did anything else, because I was too far along to do otherwise. Louis was married, though long separated from his wife. He needed a divorce. They found that the fastest legal divorce could be obtained in Mexico, where we would head if I agreed. Then he and I would be married.

On December 13, 1969, before I was formally committed to anyone or anything, labor had to be induced because there was toxemia and the baby had gone into fetal distress. He was seemingly stillborn. Suddenly there was the little stream that only a boy baby can make. The blanket was wet. My baby, a son eventually named Mark, was alive!

5

I was strolling with Mark through the lobby to our apartment
when the FBI agents asked again about my marrying Louis.
They explained that they wanted me to become the rental agent
for a luxury high rise across the street. Louis was scheduled to
become the manager, and he needed a wife working there with
him. We would be given one of the largest apartments, one with
three or four bedrooms, for my mother if she wanted to move.

We were sent to Mexico on what was dubbed the "freedom
express." This was the fastest trip for a legally accepted divorce.
Then we moved into the 32-story luxury high rise.

I had a job, good money, a beautiful building to live in, and
a friend in Louis. We were married because that was part of the
job. We would be monogamous because we took the vows as
seriously as we could, given our unusual circumstances.

The work we did was covert surveillance.

Our apartment was large, luxurious, and overlooked a
building where much of the Russian delegation was living. We
could see and photograph everyone who entered and left. The
FBI had made arrangements with housing placement at the

United Nations to steer people from the Soviet Bloc to this high rise. There were Bulgarians, Czechs, and Albanians, as well as other tenants.

The Soviet Union sent large numbers of intelligence agents to the United States, as well as members of the KGB to spy on those delegates who might defect. The Cold War was still intense, and everyone spied on everyone else. The Soviets expected us to spy on them, so we devised techniques that would undermine their expectations.

For example, a "bug" is placed under the protective plate of a power outlet. Professionals, knowing they might be bugged, routinely remove the cover, locate the bug, and destroy it or plan all their conversations around the fact that they know it exists.

Since our building was not quite finished, we wired the bugs directly behind power outlets. When the plate was removed and the socket checked, nothing would be found. Wiring the outlets meant that monitoring agents could hear everything going on in every room of the suite.

The basement held a phone room, well disguised. Two agents were there around the clock, always with recording devices. In addition, there was a van for long-range surveillance.

The knowledgeable tenants were always worried about break-ins by American agents sneaking into the building. They used tricks to determine if their suites were entered while they were at work. For example, some placed a tiny string, often an ultrathin silk, across the entrance door. The silk broke if anyone entered. If the breakage was not noticed, the silk not replaced, the tenant knew something had happened. And since the silk was so thin and so dark that it was rarely noticed, American agents breaking into the suites often left telltale signs without knowing it.

The FBI gave me a crash course in various tricks I needed to know for the spying I was doing. In addition, I joined the New York Police Auxiliary, for which I trained at John Jay College of Criminal Justice. Louis was also in the police auxiliary. To the Soviet Bloc tenants, we were just doing civic duty. We wore police uniforms and were quite open about our activities. Government agents wore business suits.

By the time I was finished with my training, I had equipment to obtain and identify fingerprints, do surveillance photography, and handle a variety of scientific and technical procedures. The idea was for me to be able to do the preliminary work normally handled by scientific investigation units. In that way I could handle certain intelligence activities without having to transfer materials to one of the police or federal labs.

We had two bathrooms in our apartment, one of which was converted into a soundproof office. The plumbing was converted so it could be used for photo processing. A large hardwood table held my direct telephone line to FBI headquarters. There was a string across the shower area on which I clipped wet documents to dry. I was trained to read blood splatters to determine how a wound was made, which way the victim had moved, and other details critical to determining the source and direction of violence. I had various training manuals for identifying guns, bullets, home loads, and reloaders. I could do basic drug testing with standard police drug identification kits.

My job included a garbage run every night. We had a trash compactor in the basement of the building. The tenants dropped their garbage down a chute where it entered the compactor. They assumed that the machinery was always in use and that it was safe to dispose of their personal memos in that way. They made little or no effort to destroy documents before dumping them.

Very late each night I went to the basement and collected

the trash. Actual garbage—food waste, empty packages, and the like—I separated out and returned to the compactor. Letters, documents, matter that seemed interesting I took to my office. I was looking for secret codes, personal notes, any information that could have political significance. The Albanian garbage was the most important. No one knew what the Albanians were doing.

Uncle Al was our contact. He arrived at the apartment around eight A.M. in order to have a cup of coffee and establish a familiar presence. He also handled our pay. Louis received his salary from the FBI, but we were each paid $500 per week for our work managing the apartment. This was fair compensation for the work that was our cover, so if anyone checked the management company's books, they would see nothing out of the ordinary.

Soviet Bloc involvement with American militant groups came out after two police officers were murdered. The officers, one black and one white, were partners on patrol. They answered a call for help in Spanish Harlem, and as they emerged from their car they were murdered by members of the Black Liberation Army, a group believed to be an offshoot of the Black Panther Party.

While going through the trash, I found a copy of a letter the Albanians had written to a college professor in the Southwest. They had provided him with $10,000 in financial support of so-called subversive antiwar groups.

One of the residents was alleged to be a Black militant leader. After the shooting of the two officers, a composite photo of one of the men seen by witnesses looked suspiciously like our tenant.

We watched the apartment. Black males came and went, tipping the doorman, driving expensive cars, yet never really staying there. It seemed to be a stop-off place. I decided I had to go in. This was what detectives call a preemptive search, done to survey potential dangers that might be faced on a subsequent entry. Inside, bullets, shell boxes, and gun belts were scattered everywhere. Magazines and extremist literature from the black militant and antiwar movements littered the floor.

Among other implements of violence, was a bullet reloader. This device was used to save money on ammunition. After bullets were fired, a bullet reloader enabled the shells to be used again. Gunpowder was inserted, then the molded lead. It could also customize a bullet, making it more powerful or perform special duty, such as splitting apart inside the victim so the organs would be ripped by shrapnel.

It was the most extreme material I had encountered working with the auxiliary. I was certain it was connected to the murder of the two cops. I called J.J. in police homicide. We went to look at the suite together.

We took a sample of shell casings from the carpet that were made with the reloader. The police forensic lab was able to prove that it had been used to make the bullets that killed the police officers. This was ultimately confirmed by the FBI lab in Washington.

The apartment next to the one under suspicion was vacant. The FBI and the police moved in. After getting a warrant and photographing everything in the black militants' suite, they waited for the occupant to turn up, arrested him, and eventually got him to give the names of the shooters. They were arrested in California within the year.

The Albanians were not arrested. They were only financial backers, and it did us more good to keep watching them, since they knew nothing about the buggings and wiretaps.

I fell into a routine. Monica went to St. Joseph's School, a short walk down the street. I would get her off, then return for the morning meeting with Uncle Al. My police scanner was constantly playing in the bathroom, and I had my direct line to the Bureau placed just below a series of wanted posters. These were FBI tools for in-house use, the subjects different from the criminal posters in post offices. They showed the various important KGB officials who were looking to stop defectors.

One of the men Uncle Al was trying to find for on-going surveillance was a KGB general we'll call Boris, a tall, handsome, high-level operative. One day he showed me a photograph of the man, explaining that he had been seeking him for months. I glanced at the picture and realized that I had rented a suite to him two weeks earlier. His daily pattern was such that I knew he would return from the mission in half an hour.

I put Mark in a stroller and we went down the elevator at the time I expected the general to return. I was several feet behind Uncle Al, who inadvertently opened the door to the mail room as Boris walked in. Boris smiled, thanked him, and went on. Then Uncle Al turned white, checked his picture again, and realized it was the same man.

I raised hell with Uncle Al for two reasons. First, the Bureau was not being as attentive as they should have been. Boris's name had been on the rental sheets. His photograph had been taken repeatedly by the surveillance cameras across the way. All the information they needed was available to them, but Al had assumed the general would never be so visible.

Even worse, Uncle Al, like most of the men who were in the FBI under J. Edgar Hoover, was eager to conform to Bureau standards. The dress code was to blend in: always appear to be an average Joe by wearing conservative clothes. Uncle Al was dressed in a suit and tie. He was also wearing a PT-109 tie pin, a gift from the Kennedy administration. Boris knew instantly where Uncle Al worked just by seeing his pin. That was why he had smiled knowingly, and that was why I was glad I was several feet behind him when Boris saw him. So long as neither Louis nor I were seen with obvious government agents, we were in the clear.

High level foreign agents often moved in with the rank and file bureaucrats or diplomats in buildings like ours to hide in the open. When I was working with the police auxiliary, we found that smart bad guys often liked to take apartments near the police stations. They assumed, rightfully, that the police would think no wanted man in his right mind would come anywhere near headquarters. The wise guys knew that the best way to hide was in plain sight.

Eventually Boris and his wife became friends with Louis and me. Louis' fluent Russian helped tremendously. We soon realized that Boris's wife was sexually interested in Louis.

Then Boris came on to me. He wanted a Seiko watch he could not buy himself, and I purchased it for him. He paid me the money to buy it, but it had to appear to be a gift. He also wanted to see Washington, D.C., which was outside the regulation 25 mile limit for Russian diplomats. I helped, working with Uncle Al to assure he was under constant surveillance.

For taking surveillance photos in the neighborhood, I had a bike with a seat for Mark. We went through the garden and around the neighborhood, taking pictures. That I happened to include one of the Albanians or other agents seemed innocent. No one saw my camera as a threat because of the two children.

I always had a pair of Minox cameras, one with me and one in my bathroom office. These are ultraminiature devices meant for use in spying. The lens is of extremely high quality, and the camera is designed for both general photography and copying documents. It can also be attached to a binocular for long distance surveillance without being obvious.

Any film that included shots of faces would be processed by

the FBI lab. The rest of the film was processed by a nearby photo store that was FBI-approved.

There were several "safe" businesses—restaurants, a travel agency, a camera shop. I was told who to trust.

The work I did for the FBI was either extremely intense or boring. My most rewarding work came from working with the New York Police Department, Twenty-third Precinct.

I was assigned to undercover work with the anticrime unit. I rode with two other detectives in a taxicab that had been converted for police use. There was a police radio. We patrolled with one man driving, the other man and I acting as passengers. We could go anywhere at any time of the day or night and seem invisible.

On my first night, we heard a report of shots fired at One hundred fifth Street. We accelerated over to the location, but we couldn't find anything. I had been drinking coffee when we went over, and I thought I had better dump it. As we drove slowly among parked cars, I poured the liquid out the window. Suddenly a man who had been on the ground sat up. He was the shooting victim. The way his body had fallen in the shadows, he could not be seen. The bullet that struck him was small enough power that it lodged in his skull instead of doing serious damage. The hot coffee splashing on him revived him, and he sat up.

The man went home six hours after receiving treatment at the hospital, refusing to stay for observation. He had apparently been involved with a drug deal gone sour.

We got a rape call one night when my partner and I were in a Twenty-third Precinct marked car, sitting along Park Avenue. The report said one victim was a white woman, another possible victim, a woman running from the scene, was Hispanic, and the suspect was a Hispanic man. We drove into the park, seeking the assailant, driving through a service lane barely wide enough to hold us.

Suddenly I saw the suspect. Instinctively, I opened the door to leap out and catch him. I made a lot of hot-headed mistakes during my time with the cops. I focused on what had to be done and did it, as did the driver I was assigned that night. We saw ourselves as good cops. The higher-ups saw us as productive nuisances who didn't screw up enough to be suspended. However, that night things were worse than usual.

My partner shouted at me to stay in the car—a moment too late. I leaped clear, drawing my gun, just as the open door smashed into a tree.

He stopped long enough for me to get back in the car, wedging the door so we could keep moving. We saw the suspect racing down the steps to the pond. We continued giving chase, driving down the steps. "We're not going to lose the son-of-a-bitch!" the driver yelled, as the car landed in the water, then died. We jumped out, split up, and chased the guy, finally catching him around Ninety-sixth Street. We handcuffed him, then had to walk him back to the precinct.

"Where's the car?" we were asked at the station.

"It's in the park," we said. "It won't start."

We caught hell for what we did. The car was totaled. The muffler was hanging down, the front smashed to hell, and the broken door had fallen off. The undercarriage was shot as well. We never admitted we did anything so dumb as driving it down the steps.

It was a nightmare for our boss. We probably should have been made responsible for the damages, but we caught the guy. Catching the bad guy counts for something.

Another night my partner and I came upon a tenement on fire while cruising in one of the unmarked vehicles for the anticrime patrol. It was a nightmare. People were screaming, flames and smoke were everywhere.

My partner liked the idea of being the first on the scene, saving lives.

We raced into one building and went to the top floor to rescue a woman and her children. The smoke was intensely thick, but we trusted our instincts as we climbed to the fifth floor.

My partner was excited. He said he knew the place where we were going to rescue the family. He had busted people there before. It was a drug den, a place where there had been stashes of drugs and cash. Once we reached the top, all that mattered to me was keeping the children from panicking as we brought them down the smoke-filled steps. We all had to stoop low, staying as close to the ground as possible so we would not be overcome by the smoke.

Back outside I was choking, I couldn't breathe. The fire was out of control, but the woman and her children were safe. However, when I turned around to check on my partner, to my horror I found he had not followed. Sick, choking, I had to climb back up to the fifth floor where I found him semiconscious.

Now the smoke was thicker. I was getting dizzy, trying to slide on my stomach down the steps, dragging him with me. Fortunately the fire department arrived as I was passing out from the smoke. We both ended in Metropolitan Hospital, and it was only a matter of luck that we weren't killed.

Louis and I tried to work our police department schedules around the kids. Mama lived in a brownstone next door, and she helped me with Mark. Monica came home from school at three o'clock, and I was always there for her. Anyone interested saw a normal working family.

Nights were spent with the police. Louis and I went to the precinct around 7 P.M. while my mother sat with the kids. Louis went on patrol. I went to the squad room where I had a desk with a special telephone.

I set up files for crimes according to types—arson, burglary, armed robbery, rape, etc. I also set up files on criminals according to physical appearance. It enabled us to locate people and connect them with crimes more efficiently.

But the real reason I was sitting there was to expedite the special calls originating from the Soviet Bloc residents of the building Louis and I managed.

If the break-in was detected, the resident would report it to Louis, if he was home, or my mother, when she was sitting with the kids.

My mother's role was to be extremely sympathetic and concerned when a break-in was reported. She wanted to know if anything was taken, if anything needed to be done to help. Always she would insist on giving a full police report to the Twenty-third Precinct. Then she would use my red phone to the FBI and let them know what happened.

Eventually the call from the tenant would go to the department and be transferred to me. I would change my accent to one that was somewhat southern, with a nasal twang. I was patient, calm, taking all the details. I would mix business with a touch of sympathy, explaining that two of our best detectives would be sent over as fast as possible.

Then two well-briefed detectives would take a #61 Criminal Complaint Report, fingerprint kit, and other items over to the location of the break-in. The FBI made certain the detectives understood their roles. They were to be serious, professional, compassionate, and go through the motions of checking everything they could. Naturally, the crime would always go unsolved.

There was never anything taken. However, the people were reassured by the way the matter was handled. They did not realize that everyone they encountered, even the detectives handling their complaints, was working with the FBI.

Experiencing damage allowed the Soviets to relax. They realized that the person was probably a druggie searching for something that could be sold for fast cash. The area was known for having junkies. There was a door to the front, two entrances to the garage, and a service entrance. The diplomats and intelligence personnel, aware of the street people just outside the building, could understand the problem. Naturally we were sympathetic, sometimes telling them how we had improved security in the building, sometimes claiming we had thrown out suspicious individuals.

One problem we had in the high rise was with rats. Apparently a mistake was made when the building was being completed and a rats' nest was sealed in the wall.

Mark was nineteen months old when I discovered the problem. I awakened one night to find blood on Mark and a nipple chewed off a bottle near his bed. There had been some milk on his cheek, and a rat had gotten on his bed, biting him to eat it off.

I found a rat in the closet, knew what had happened, and went crazy. I tried to stop Mark's bleeding, then got a shotgun and went after the rat. I saw that the rats were using the air conditioning duct and I blasted that. Finally I pulled off the duct. There was the nest, filled with chewed dollar bills and other pieces of paper.

The problem was more serious than anyone realized. The building was infested through the first six floors. The health department wanted to close down the entire structure, but if they did, an important operation would be compromised. Government security required eradicating the problem without losing the tenants.

Mark developed what the doctors called rat bite fever. When he was placed in pediatric intensive care he was semicomatose, had malaise, and a high fever. He was listed in critical condition, and I stayed by his side for a week. For months after he went home, the sore on his face would periodically break out.

The air-conditioning ducts for all floors were sealed. The health department inspector was outraged. The correction work was extremely expensive. Fortunately we did not have a problem keeping the tenants.

Ironically, Mark's infection was healed by a Russian Mission doctor who handled the medical needs for the UN personnel of the Soviet Mission. She had worked in Cuba and other parts of Latin America, spoke several languages, and was as beautiful as she was brilliant. She provided a topical ointment for his face from her stock of Soviet medicines. I don't know if rat bites were more prevalent in Latin America than in the United States, but I do know it worked.

Uncle Al took a small sampling of the cream to have analyzed. The medicinal properties were better than anything we had in this country. The analysis was sent to a lab and eventually the medication was duplicated by one of the American pharmaceutical manufacturers.

For her services, the Russian physician requested a Bible. Always watched by a KGB agent, she was forbidden to enter a bookstore, but she could order books by mail. I arranged for her to get a cookbook she wanted, a Bible, and other items. With the approval of Uncle Al, our FBI case agent, I put her on the mailing list for the U.S. Government Printing Office.

The Soviets were permitted to give and receive gifts, so we made whatever purchases they wanted, and then "gave" the items as presents. It did not matter how many material goods they took back with them so long as they were not caught actually spending money in this country.

Because of the mail orders, Monica and Mark received an FBI file number. At twenty-two months, Mark was toddling and delighted in carrying a package to the Russians' apartment. Because of the thoroughness of our surveillance, his actions were duly noted. I pointed out that he could not be a part of the operation, which included delivering the packages, unless he received a 201 Active File, becoming the youngest paid civilian in FBI history.

6

For several years Louis and I played the game of spying on our tenants, their friends, and their business associates.

One day when my mother was watching a report on the Watergate break-ins, I saw E. Howard Hunt, who I had known as Eduardo, and my old assassination coach and CIA brigade instructor, Frank Sturgis, being led away, perhaps to jail. That caught my attention.

It turned out Sturgis was sentenced to a penitentiary in Danbury, Connecticut. He had spent years doing work for the White House in one form or another. He had been in Cuba, had fought for and against Castro. He had taken an assignment as a wire and breaking and entering man for the Nixon reelection campaign. He may have been a killer. He may have been corrupt. He may have been a lot of things. But he considered himself a patriot and expected a pardon.

Frustrated and angry, feeling betrayed by the those who employed him, Sturgis got in touch with the New York *Daily News*. He wanted to tell the story of his past. One day our doorman told me that a reporter for the paper had arrived at the apartment looking for Marita Lorenz. I told the doorman I didn't know her, but eventually after getting agency clearance, I talked with the reporter. He explained that he was running a story written with Frank Sturgis, and he needed to talk with me. He told me about the articles and said they were going to print the following week.

The reporter had photographs from Sturgis that included a picture of me with Fidel that the cruise photographer had taken on the *M.S. Berlin* in Cuba in 1959. There was no question that if the story ran, it would blow my cover. I would no longer be of any value to the FBI. I was convinced that this was conceived by a CIA agent we will call Tom in order to get me back.

The FBI went after the *Daily News*, trying desperately to kill the story. Everything about the time in Florida, my time with Fidel, the portion of my life I did not want to remember, was laid out in scrupulous detail. I was furious. After fifteen years of clandestine life, Watergate was about to blast the lid off.

I arranged to talk with Sturgis in the penitentiary. He acted as though he was talking to an old friend. I was outraged, swearing at him. "Why did you tell them about me?" I asked him. Knowing that we were probably both being tape recorded, he ignored that, not saying anything about any covert operations. I asked him if he had killed Alex and Camilo. He laughed and said the CIA did it.

Frank explained that he was not supposed to be in jail. We both worked for the government. There were things we both expected that had not come through for him. Then he admitted he had used me as a fall guy and suggested that I use the publicity to make money.

Eventually Frank was shipped to a prison in the Washington, D.C. area. At the same time, the six-part series was heavily advertised. There was promotional material about "Marita Lorenz, Superspy." They also had information about Fidel keeping a bazooka under the bed on which we made love. But nothing could prepare me for the day that Monica and I went to a newsstand on Eighty-sixth Street and saw the paper's headlines: HER CIA ORDERS: KILL FIDEL. While I was more than fifteen years older than in the photograph, anyone reading the paper would recognize me. Maybe this was the CIA's way of destroying my usefulness with the FBI. Maybe this was Sturgis' way to get back at me.

Sturgis eventually sold his story to a variety of publications, and I was frequently mentioned. He became as famous for what he might have done as for what he had been caught doing or confessed to doing. He was a hot property, and I heard rumors that there were years when his income was in the six figures for the stories he sold. The only thing to which he did not confess was being a shooter in the Kennedy assassination, though he never denied it. There was just no way of knowing if he was being coy for the press or protecting himself from prosecution for the one crime for which there was no statute of limitations.

The day the story hit it was all over—the work for the FBI, the marriage to Louis, the undercover operation. We had failed to understand how vicious and self-centered the contract CIA players could be.

I was intensely depressed. I left the kids with my mother, then walked, crying, to the East River. I stood by the railing and looked at the flat boats. I felt deceived. Tears streamed down my face. I hated Sturgis, wanted to kill him. I hated the American press for invading my privacy. They hadn't even offered me a chance to defend myself. They just published, not giving a damn about the impact of their words on so many lives.

As I looked at the water, an old man out with his dog was sitting on a park bench feeding the pigeons. "Don't cry," he told me. "You're too pretty to cry. And don't jump. You'll ruin my day."

I convinced him that I was upset, not suicidal. I asked him if he knew of any apartments for rent in the area. Ironically he was the superintendent of a building on East Eighty-eighth Street. He said that he had a small garden apartment available, so we went there and I rented it on the spot. At least I still had plenty of cash. I got the key, went in, and sat down in the middle of the floor.

The Soviet bloc tenant also realized that with the super of the building working for the Feds, it was time to move on. They relocated within the month.

It was February 1976. Louis and I divorced. I did not know what the future would bring, though I knew I wanted to get even.

V

THE
WHOLE
TRUTH

1

After the *Daily News* story came out, Congress established the House of Representatives Select Committee on Assassinations to investigate all covert actions by the CIA and other government agencies. Men I had known over the years were becoming increasingly nervous about what was going to take place. Members of organized crime wondered if they would be victims of the probe, targets for destruction to prevent the public knowing about their connections with "legitimate" politicians.

Johnny Roselli, a.k.a. Mr. Hollywood, was ordered to testify concerning his knowledge of the Kennedy assassination. He became frightened of what would happen if he talked. Before he could tell what he knew, plead the Fifth Amendment or perjure himself as Santo Trafficante did, his decision was made for him. He was murdered.

In October 1977 Frank Sturgis and I talked about the House assassination probe. We were sceptical of each other for what each of us thought were good and valid reasons. I felt he wanted to influence or silence me to prevent me from testifying about covert activities. He felt I was a traitor to what he believed to be the "cause." He also wanted me working full–time for the CIA.

Sturgis had been jailed as a participant in the Watergate break–in. He had repeatedly been named by writers and investigators looking into the Kennedy assassination as a conspiracy. Some were aware that he had been actively involved with the attempts to overthrow Fidel Castro from 1959 on.

Frank and I talked after I met with the Congressional committee's investigators to inform them about covert activities and the Dallas trip. When Sturgis and I discussed the testimony I had given and my refusal to go to Angola, I came to the conclusion that he was setting me up, based not only on what he said but from knowing him over the years.

Sturgis claimed he never threatened me, and ultimately, after reviewing seven different tapes of telephone conversations we had, Judge Erwin Torres, a Criminal Court Judge in Manhattan, agreed. In addition, Sturgis and his attorney claimed that I had paid for him to fly from Miami to New York to see me that October 1977.

Following our conversation about the committee interview I had given, I was angry. I cursed Sturgis to Inspector Francis X. Smith. Anger upset Monica. Unknown to me, later that evening she listened to the tape of Sturgis' latest call. Monica was fifteen at the time, a student at the Loyola School on Park Avenue.

On Halloween, Sturgis was coming to talk to me. Instead of going to school, Monica changed into jeans, rented a semiautomatic pistol from associates she knew, took her passport and some money, and waited by a brownstone across the street.

Monica called me from a phone booth to let me know her plans. She wouldn't listen to reason, insisting she would save me. I called my friend, police inspector Smith who in turn called the Twenty-third Precinct.

When Sturgis got out of a cab, she started shooting. Her

first shots missed, thank God. After that, she ran, crying, terrified.

While the police from the Twenty-third Precinct, where I had worked, tried to seal her in a two-block area, Monica began leaping from rooftop to rooftop until she made her way near to the Mayor's mansion on East 88th Street and East End Avenue. There she entered the yard, where a police department guard had a booth and phone.

Monica called me from a telephone booth by the Mayor's mansion. She wanted to know if she had hit Sturgis; she just wanted to scare him away from me. I was desperate to have her forget Frank and turn herself in.

The police prepared a stand off. Hostage negotiation cops were called in. A three-block area at East End and York Avenues was cordoned off. There were officers on an adjoining roof with assault rifles.

Monica understood that the police did not want to hurt her, but they could not let someone armed and potentially dangerous onto the crowded Manhattan streets. She'd been around police all her life; they were my coworkers and friends. She called for "Uncle Terry" (Detective Terry McSwiggin) and surrendered to him.

Frank was arrested on a charge of coercion. His bail was set at $25,000, and he had to spend time in Rikers Island jail. The police felt that he was going to attempt to force me to change my testimony—the whole truth—I told the investigator and I would tell the House Assassinations Committee.

Monica was released to my custody after being arraigned at the criminal court, youth division. As a result of her actions, she was dismissed from Loyola and disgraced on the front page of the *Daily News*.

Harassment began. The day after Roselli was found murdered, someone slipped a newspaper under my door. It featured the headline of the murder, under which somebody wrote the words "You're next." Ironically, at one point I met the shooter who had been contracted to kill me, who broke down and admitted he had been unable to do it to someone so much like himself.

I believe that most of the violence and severe aggravated harassment in my life came from the CIA or was CIA-related. However, I had also been in routine police work as well as FBI intelligence. As Frank Sturgis warned me, I "had hit too many bases." I was always a target due to my unwanted Fidel headlines. If the CIA has a contract on you, moving or running doesn't help. If they want to kill, they will.

I confided in a longtime friend, Shelly Abend, who owned a horse farm in upstate New York and had long been involved in the intelligence community. He knew my background and expressed concern for my safety. He arranged for me to talk with an attorney, Jim Garrison, who had been involved in investigating the Kennedy assassination as a conspiracy. Shelly was instrumental in placing me under protective custody until attempts against my life were called off.

The day the custody began was a comedy of errors. I had a longtime friend from my club-hopping days. "Chow Māin" was a user of recreational drugs, someone who liked living in the fast lane, party, party, party. She stopped by my apartment to visit and began making telephone calls to friends from my place. The Marshals realized she was a security risk. She was told she would have to come into custody, too.

I couldn't explain to Chow that she was going to be placed under whatever form of custody was necessary to keep her from more phone calls. Rather than having her become hysterical, I asked her if she would like to come on a vacation with me. I said we would be going to the Bahamas where she could enjoy herself and dry out.

Chow was quite wired on stimulants. She was mad at her latest boyfriend and a vacation sounded perfect. She agreed to go, and within a couple of hours we were on a plane south, destination unknown.

We were kept in federal protective custody in Miami Springs Villa, a compound near the Miami airport. There were several cottages that were quite secluded.

We drove in an official vehicle with tinted window glass. The cottage was kept shuttered at all times. There were two plain clothes guards armed for security, one of whom was a woman.

One night when I was sleeping, I felt something on my neck. It was a light pressure, though enough so I became half awake. When I opened my eyes, I saw a naked man holding a knife to my neck. He used enough pressure so I was aware of the point. There was no question in my mind that I was going to die. "Holy Shit! My God!" I was filled with pure terror. My mind raced to evaluate and handle this.

The intruder was whispering to me, telling me the sexually violent things he was going to do to me. He was sweating profusely, panting, mumbling, urging: white male, approximately twenty-seven years, five feet eight inches, blonde, blue eyes, 185 pounds. This naked stranger was deadly, a disturbed sexual deviate.

The words he was using were disgustingly descriptive. He was holding his penis with one hand, the knife—a sharp, double-edged stiletto—in the other. Each time he stroked himself, his body moved enough so the blade lightly punctured my skin.

I was not allowed to carry my gun with me to Florida. But I never went unarmed. I had as usual, a switchblade knife in the

215

back pocket of my jeans. The pants were at the foot of the bed. I quietly convinced him to go into the other room with me. I said that I didn't want to awaken anyone else. I talked to him quietly, edged him backwards out the door. I slipped the knife out of my pocket, flicked the blade open, and cut him superficially on the wrist.

I began jumping from side to side, edging him out, moving him, keeping from being an easy target, looking for an opening. Then I saw Monica coming from her bedroom. She began screaming, "Mommy! Mommy!" Chow also awakened and began screaming.

I shouted to Monica to go back. I shouted at Chow to shut up. I wanted to keep him moving backward out the door.

I slashed, the blade ripping at his chest, his arms. He fell backwards over a coffee table, righted himself and headed for the door.

I maneuvered him out the door, forced it shut, and began barricading it with my left hand, still clutching the knife in the other. Mark walked into the room, frightened. Monica alternated between trying to comfort him and helping to barricade the doors.

Finally I used my left hand to slap Chow across the face to get her to calm down. She stopped screaming and started crying. "They're coming to kill us!" she said. "They're coming to kill us!"

"He's a nut, Chow," I told her. "Get the phone and call Steve." Steve was my case agent, to whom we had a direct line.

Chow was terrified. She was too hysterical to be of use, Mark was too young to be a part of this. I was splattered with blood, though unhurt.

Monica went to the telephone calmly, lifted the receiver, and asked for Steve as soon as the monitor picked up. Someone got on the telephone, and Monica communicated the danger.

Meanwhile I desperately looked for any weapons that might have been hidden by the marshals, but there were none.

The man began sticking his blade through the jalousies covering the bathroom window. He was trying to come inside. "I'm going to kill you. Let me in. You hurt me. You're a bad girl."

The slashing sounds continued. He began going from window to window, using his knife to probe the slats of the jalousies trying to force a space where he could place his hand and open it.

Chow was out of control. She finally curled up in a ball of fear. Mark raced to the bed and threw the covers over his head. Monica stayed with him, covering his ears with her hands, terrified yet trying to protect her brother.

Finally help arrived. There were six or eight officers, guns drawn, and emergency medical personnel.

I sat down stunned, unable to let go of the knife. Steve's face was white, shocked.

Monica was given a shot to help her calm down. I comforted the children, talked to them, cuddled them. This was the most traumatic event in my children's lives.

"What was he wearing?" Steve asked.

"Pubic hair and a knife," I replied.

Mark, eight years old, came out from under the covers and calmly said, "Oh, just another day in the life of old Mom." Then he asked one of the marshals for some promised ice cream and books.

We were moved immediately to a hotel near the airport. We were given the honeymoon suite with a massive sunken bathtub, a balcony, and television. We got oysters, steak, or anything else we wanted.

A search began immediately. They followed the bloody trail.

217

It was several weeks before they identified and jailed our assailant.

My absent guards were given hell.

The last part of our time in protective custody was dedicated to my writing about the Dallas trip in "The Green Book," a green notebook provided by Steve. I was to cover everything from the meeting with Fidel to my involvement with the Cuban exiles, Operation 40, and the drive to Dallas. I was to name names and tell exactly what I knew. There was to be no conjecture. I was to tell in my own words exactly what had taken place in my association with the CIA. My information would be read by the House Assassination Committee members.

They were concerned with the activities alleged against Sturgis. Frank was a CIA contract employee. They suspected he had been involved with all manner of illegal activities.

Sturgis had been caught in a number of different ways, and various intelligence agencies felt there was more to it. However, there was nothing I actually witnessed for which the statute of limitations had not expired, or charges could be brought. When he appeared on television shows, talking about the Kennedy assassination, he would play coy speaking only of his patriotic duties for national security. He would neither take responsibility for any violence, nor insist upon his innocence.

2

I was subpoenaed by the Select Committee on Assassinations. On May 1, 1978, just before I testified in closed executive session hearings, I was given a document that stated:

Order Conferring Immunity Upon and Compelling Testimony From Merita (sic) Lorenz

The United States House of Representatives Select Committee on Assassinations having made written application, pursuant to Title 18, United States Code, Sections 6002 and 6005, for an order conferring immunity upon Merita Lorenz and compelling her to testify and provide other information before the Subcommittee on the assassination of John F. Kennedy of the Select Committee on Assassinations, and the court finding that all procedures specified by S 6005 have been duly followed, it is hereby, this 1st of May, 1978, ORDERED, that Merita Lorenz [Marita Lorenz was hand written as a correction] in accordance with the provisions of Title 18, United States Code, Sections 6002 and 6005, shall not be excused from testifying or providing other information before the Subcommittee on the Assassination of John F. Kennedy of the Select Committee on Assassinations on the grounds that the testimony or other information sought may tend to incriminate her."

219

The form said that, in addition to the Kennedy case, I had
to

testify and provide such other information that is sought with
respect to matters under inquiry by said Subcommittee.

AND IT IS FURTHER ORDERED that no testimony or
other information compelled under this order or any information
directly or indirectly derived from such testimony or other
information may be used against Merita Lorenz in any criminal
case, except a prosecution for perjury, giving a false statement
or otherwise failing to comply with this ORDER.

It was signed by United States District Judge William B.
Bryant.

When I was subpoenaed, I wanted to take off. I'd had
enough of the government, enough of death threats and harassment, enough of protection that placed my family in danger.
But there was no escaping the subpoena. In any case, it was my
duty.

I knew what I was facing. My early childhood had been
made a nightmare because of the war. Then I was raped by the
sergeant with the occupation forces. I had been abducted,
aborted, almost died in Cuba with Castro. Then the horror with
Marcos, then Sturgis. One way or another, I stayed stigmatized
with a past full of violence that I could not shake. I had,
hopefully, learned something from it all. I was prepared to face
the music, whatever the tune.

Individuals who had been connected with the CIA, such as
Johnny Roselli, were being professionally murdered, maybe to
silence them. About this time I was approached by Tom Guinzburg at Viking. He told me that by talking, by doing a book, I
would gain exposure that could keep me alive.

I wasn't sure what I wanted to do, but I did begin going
through my boxes of personal memorabilia. I looked at scrap-

books, boxes of photographs, and numerous documents I had accumulated.

While on assignment, I had been trained to say nothing about what we were doing. This was in the best interests of national security. We participated actively in gun running. I had been involved with deaths during training exercises. I was fairly certain that one or more people had been eliminated during the time when I was a member of Op 40. I helped to "borrow" yachts worth hundreds of thousands of dollars. I had led a life above the law—in the service of the United States of America.

For years I had been protected by and associated with men at the top. Congress had allowed massive sums of money to be spent for covert action without any accountability. They either assumed that everything was being done in the best interests of the country, or they feared going against the CIA.

Now I felt that it was my duty to alert the American people to the truth about what the CIA was doing. The people of the United States were asking questions. They would no longer dismiss my charges out of fear or disbelief. They would listen, if nothing else, provided all files were released.

Monica, Mark, and our two Bichon puppies accompanied me when I went to Washington to testify. We were guarded, secreted in a hotel just outside the city, then brought in by marshals. Tom Guinzburg supplied a lawyer to help assure my rights as a witness. I wore a three-piece suit ordered off a truck from associates who were "committed."

I entered the committee hearing room, the children and pups right behind me. I was shown my various exhibits, including the green notebook in which I had been writing. That was Exhibit #1.

I opened the notebook in order to identify the exhibit. I

noticed that it had been tampered with. There were names added, and other names or details scratched out in some places, altered in others. "Hey, somebody fucked with it!" I said, not knowing the microphone in front of me was on. My words carried on the sound system, much to my embarrassment. "Look. I didn't write that. Look, they wrote it over."

The committee members sat staring at me, stunned by my outburst.

I was given a minute to identify my writing. Most of the writing that was altered was about covert activities and associates in the CIA.

The committee had obtained, as Exhibit #2, materials taken from my apartment during illegal search and seizure sometime when I was in protective custody. These were old address books and similar materials from the 1960s. Inside were names, telephone numbers, codes. CIA station chiefs were listed by name and address. There were personal telephone numbers for agents. It was information only someone who was a part of the events of those days could have. Also entered were my photographs, extradition papers, the trust fund documents. I felt like my life was public record.

The committee members were obviously seeking anything that linked the Miami anti-Castro Cubans with assassinations and covert activities. They were especially interested in the trips to New Orleans I had taken, as well as addresses there. One address connected a number of men who ultimately proved to be involved with either the CIA, the Mafia, or both.

Other personal documents placed in evidence were internal communications and citations from both the FBI and the CIA; these were proofs of employment, as were the serial numbers of my weapons. Other documents detailed espionage materials I had used in my work. These included at least one Minox camera, a variety of films, adapters, an enlarger, a fingerprint dust kit, as well as a variety of IDs and passports with different names and backgrounds. I had put these things in a suitcase and turned them over to the N.Y.P.D. and FBI.

The case also contained a radio transceiver, a tape recorder, invisible ink, a one-handed loupe magnifier, CIA manuals for assassination, pens and pencils, and several audio tapes of recorded telephone conversations.

The tapes proved embarrassing for the N.Y.C. police chief who had been my confidant and lover. On one tape I was trying to convince him to give up his golf game so we could fool around. On another, he said, "Fuck the department. I'm coming over."

To both the Congressional Committee's investigators and the New York Police Internal Affairs Division, the documentation was fascinating. Everything I had was meant to be used solely by legitimate law enforcement officers for legitimate activities.

I told the Committee the details of what had taken place. I explained about meeting Castro, what I had witnessed, and what I had heard that I believed to be accurate, to the best of my ability.

I told them I believed that the President did not solely run the country. The "Company" could do whatever it desired in the '60s, as long as we didn't get caught by locals, if it came under national security.

I testified that the CIA often passed disinformation and misinformation as "fact." I explained that money appropriated for clandestine operations financed covert actions probably a violation of international treaties, and extravagant expenses, even outright theft because there was no accountability.

The House Assassination Committee report was not released. The participants were uncertain. Frank Sturgis, who had testified before one committee after another since the time of the Warren Report, steadfastly claimed to have been home with his wife in Miami on the 22nd, something I could not disprove. But my testimony, and those of others who had similar backgrounds, helped end the complacency that had allowed rogue agents literally to get away with murder.

3

I continued to experience the deadly harassment that began in 1977—nightmare after nightmare. I suspected the CIA was responsible.

In October 1979, when Castro came to speak at the United Nations, Secret Service agents told me to leave the country. I was living at 86 Maywood Road in Darien, Connecticut. A few days before Castro arrived, my home was shot up and a number of my animals—ducks, pigs, horses, goats—were killed.

I got Monica and Mark into our '78 Seville and fled to Montreal, Canada, where I drove up to the Cuban Embassy and asked for protection. I was followed by armed agents, who waited for me outside the mission for two days while I pleaded for protection. Finally I left the mission and fled back to my New York apartment at 512 East Eighty-eighth Street. The agents tailing me tried to run me off the road. They fired, and I fired back.

My apartment had been ransacked and fire bombed. There was no electricity. My children were terrified. For six weeks we lived in the dark, cold apartment. My nine-year-old son set up a hibachi on the floor for heat and cooking. I had no money and had to sell my possessions, from saddles to citations, on the street. After six weeks, we were evicted.

In the eyes of the CIA agents who were after me, I was a nonperson with no rights. It did not matter to them that I was a mother with children. They had no mercy. Every time I and my children entered a Cuban mission to try to defect to Cuba, I was tailed by intelligence officials and threatened with death.

Finally, in March 1980, I was told to report to One Police Plaza in Manhattan, where a CIA agent gave me an option: "you can either go into the next room and blow your brains out, or take care of the Marielitos your fucking boyfriend is dumping on U.S. shores." He handed me a .38. My nine-year-old son Mark told him, "Mom's not going to blow her brains out." I signed a blank CIA paper, joined army intelligence, and went to Fort Indiantown Gap, Pennsylvania.

The Marielitos, the Cuban boat people, were being ware-housed in the massive reserve military base at Ft. Indiantown Gap, Pennsylvania, near Ft. Meade. It was a secluded training center used most frequently by the National Guard, but also by the National Security Agency and the Central Intelligence Agency, when needed.

At first my duty was to act as translator/investigator for the new Cubans passing through In-Processing. I was officially a part of military intelligence. I was to discover who had passports, then collect them. That would prevent easy passage back and forth to Cuba. I was also to determine which of the refugees spoke German, Russian, Czech, French, or other languages that might indicate these individuals had been to East Germany and were probably former trusted Angola military graduates.

I brought the refugees cigarettes and talked with them casually in their barracks. They shared experiences with me, and it would become obvious which ones were well-traveled and thus might be of higher rank. The U.S. wanted to know who among them might be spies or potential terrorists, and who might be able to provide additional intelligence on the Cuban government to U.S. Intelligence officials where young soldiers had been sent overseas (Angola), as well as with whom and how they were fighting, could be important information.

I wore military garb, but I tried to wear it out of regulation at times. I kept a pistol on my desk, not in my holster as was standard. The Marielitos knew I was military, but they also sensed that I was knowledgeable about Cuba and sympathetic. The fact that there might be a search-seizure weapons raid on their barracks after we talked never seemed to alert them about me.

Many had to be detoxed to get them off the tranquilizers they had taken when they left Cuba for the United States. Drugs for anxiety were free in Cuba.

Everyone had a file that was color coded according to sexual orientation and other factors. These files were used to separate families from single males, single females, children who were orphaned or otherwise without parents, homosexuals, criminals, and the like. The barracks, originally equipped to handle only single males, were divided and fenced off into separate areas.

As more and more refugees arrived, the situation became ovecrowded and tense at Fort Indiantown Gap. Buses arrived daily from Miami. The bus runs seemed to never end.

The Eighty-second Airborne was there, as was the INS Delta Detention Force. There were translators, security personnel, military construction personnel.

We had to establish order. Our attitude for enforcement was "We're here to help you, but if you don't follow the rules, we'll beat the shit out of you." We were benign terrorists at best in the eyes of many. They were taught in Cuba to fear the U.S. military. Rightfully so.

Sometimes the detainees had no intention of causing trouble. They were humble, polite, and helpful. But some of the detainees so resented us as a deterrant in their long frustrating wait for freedom that they fought us every step of the way.

We had not been told that many of the Marielitos deported to the United States were ex-prisoners. Mostly acts of hooliganism landed them in Cuban jails. However, Fidel's definition of someone who should be jailed and deported was much more rigid than slack U.S. standards. He demanded "discipline."

For example, there was the 19-year-old boy who had written anti-Castro slogans, like SCREW FIDEL, on the wall of a public building with a can of spray paint. He was from a middle class family. His mother worked in a store. His father was in the army. And the price he paid, in addition to a loss of freedom, was to have an identification number tattooed on the lower part of his lip. His future had been bleak in Cuba. His future in the United States was no better, if not worse.

The tattoos were consistent for everyone who had been in jail. It did not disfigure the face, though it was carried for life.

The gays were ostracized and jailed in Cuba if caught together on a public beach. They were not accepted or tolerated.

Fidel wanted orderliness. There was no place for anyone who could not conform. What we would consider normal adolescent rebellion he did not tolerate in any way. He was a total disciplinarian who desired respect. He saw those individuals who were lazy, criminal, demanding, or rebellious as counter revolutionaries.

The exprisoners we encountered were mostly political, rarely rapists, robbers, or other felons. They simply did not conform to Castro's society. However, our mistreatment resulted in some of them becoming criminals after arriving in the U.S.

One of the men I met was a tall, blond, distant relative and neighbor of Raúl Castro. He was well educated, extremely intelligent, spoke three languages fluently, but he was gay. He was sponsored in the community by a seemingly respectable businessman in Arkansas. The upstanding citizen was involved with gay sadomasochism and pornography and wanted to use the Cuban as a "model." The young man returned to the base completely abused, beaten, and raped, and was hospitalized.

The screening of sponsors was handled by overworked Red Cross and other professionals. Many of the staff people were young, with good intentions. They wanted to help as many people as possible become free from confinement, but tried to follow guidelines. They saw in the would-be sponsors individuals as loving and caring as themselves. Then they became aware that someone offering to help another person might have an ulterior motive. The truth was that some sponsors were often seeking cheap labor, a live-in babysitter, a sex object with whom to enjoy their favored perversion, someone they could exploit. These were individuals with money, often politically well-connected, and able to hide their private lives.

It happened often enough that procedures should have been altered, the screening process improved. Tragically, no one in a position of authority monitored how the Cubans were sponsored once out on the streets of the U.S.

There were other problems as well. Lonely American women learned that 100,000 men were involved in the detention process over time—black, brown, and white men, tall, short, fat, and thin men. The women were like hordes of hungry, prepaid diners lined up outside an all-you-can-eat buffet as the doors were opened. They knew that everywhere they looked, they would find something they thought would end their emptiness.

The women met the men in many different ways. Some hung around the gates, striking up conversations when possible. Some had family conections who gave them the name of a

detainee. Others brought friends and friends of friends. Whatever the case, romances developed, at least in the minds of the
women. They sponsored the men they met in various ways,
sometimes setting them up in an apartment, at other times
bringing them into their homes.

The women knew nothing of the men, nothing of their past
or their mental state. Just as many of the detainees were
exploited, so were a number of the women sponsors. Some of
the relationships proved successful. Some of the men married
long enough to get the American identification material they
needed to obtain work, then left for parts unknown with their
new Social Security numbers. Others raped the women, and
turned to crime. There were even deliberate murders and
beatings that led to the deaths of some of the women sponsors.

The Cubans often downplayed or exaggerated their past.
One man told me he was an artist who could not get work in
Cuba. There was no check to see what skills he had. Instead,
an effort was made to place him where he could use his
unproven, unknown skills, like making deadly weapons.

Some of the soldiers in Castro's army came from the war
being fought in Angola. They were well-trained, then became
disillusioned. A few of these graduates from Angola had unusual African diseases so foreign to U.S. medics that they
became isolated studies in tropical diseases. Among the worst
were the men with long worms under their skins. The white
worms force themselves out of openings in the arms, then have
to be fully removed by a physician. The sufferer was then
quarantined, as were those having rare blood diseases. If a
sponsor appeared for any of the quarantined men, they would
be "cured" quickly by some sort of stimulant to make them
appear healthy. Then they became the responsibility of the
sponsor, as well as the community at large.

All of us working there had to get massive inoculations—

5000 cc's of penicillin monthly. Most were intramuscular, which meant we had trouble sitting.

Several of us wondered if the release of the sick men increased the spread of unknown tropical diseases or immune deficiency illness. There was no follow-up on those who were sponsored out.

I spent approximately eight months at Fort Indiantown Gap. We were listed as the Cuban/Haitian Relocation Program of the U.S. State Department, but there were no Haitians there. The Cuban refugees were political refugees. The Haitians were economic refugees. The U.S. funding was being given to us as though we had both, since there appeared to be more national sympathy for the Haitians.

The U.S. State Department, the Department of Health and Human Services, FBI, CIA, and INS were involved with the refugees, the responsibility going back and forth among them. It was difficult to find anyone who understood who was in charge, as the Marielitos grew to 125,000 plus.

The decision was made to ship the refugees to Arkansas. I was given twenty-four hours to transfer with them. I was met at Fort Smith by Base Camp Director Gunther Wagner, then went on to Fort Chaffee Military Base.

Fort Chaffee had a better, warmer climate and was larger than Fort Indiantown Gap; it was better prepared to receive the influx of refugees. The D.C. Park Police, the Eighty-second Airborne, federal marshals, local law enforcement for crowd control were enlisted to help with the detainees. Spanish-speaking law-enforcement officers were asked to help interpret. Most of the interpreters were Mexican, and decent warm officers.

The Red Cross and other charitable agencies continued to be involved, along with Army personnel as well as the International Rescue Committee. The agencies were overwhelmed, struggling, through barriers of language and custom, to understand the problems and needs before providing clothing and supplies, often either the wrong type or in excess of what was needed.

I became a troubleshooter with the Cubans. I was almost fluent in their language and customs. These were Cubans who had experienced more than twenty-five years of Castro's power. Many were born in '59, when Castro took over, and had known him their entire lives. Many were named after Fidel. Others were older, had experienced both Fidel and Batista.

In many instances these individuals had been loyal to the Cuban government, then found that they were being deported to a country they had rightfully been told was their enemy. They were people who had been led to believe they would enter the mainstream. Suddenly they were in a barbed wire detention center, overcrowded, without adequate recreation or education facilities. Normal individuals mingled with the mentally ill and the occasionally violent criminal. Many were treated without respect and expected to communicate with people who did not speak their language.

Eventually the pressures of boredom and hopelessness became overwhelming for some of them. They formed gangs according to Cuban provinces that fought each other. They got involved with religious rituals of one sort or another. They made trouble. Because I was one of the few people present with any prior experience with Cubans, I was asked to help quell the disturbances, riots, and disputes.

Often the problems were avoidable and readily correctable. For example, a homosexual might try to have sex with a younger boy. Removing the homosexual would resolve the problem. I would arrange for the segregation.

Many of the refugees practiced Santeria, a religion that is a mixture of Afro-Cuban Catholicism and what U.S. authorities felt was voodoo. There were occasional animal sacrifices. Most followers kept some sort of religious shrine by their bunks. Usually this would consist of religious items (the Virgin and Child) and an assortment of offerings, ranging from Fidel's picture to cookies, toothpaste tubes from the Red Cross (from those people who had nothing), an orange, or flowers. Besides the Virgin, there were various goddesses, such as the goddess "Omaya."

Barracks were militarily in order. There were twenty-four or more to each barracks. While everything was neat, for the Cubans were meticulously neat, the shrines were upsetting to the guards. During raids, the guards would take their batons and smash the shrines, much to the shock and sadness of the Marielitos. Whenever that occurred, there was a high risk of rioting and retaliation fighting. It was unnecessary.

Once a week there would be careful sweeps for concealed homemade weapons. Often a former Cuban prison guard might bunk in the same location as a former inmate. This would create the potential for violence, fighting and squabbling, until I relocated them.

One man was a severe manic-depressive who wanted to go back to Cuba. He was suicidal, and the guards had no idea what to do with him. They did not speak Spanish, so they were limited to either letting him take his own life or somehow restraining him. Even worse, he was constantly trying to escape from the base. I was brought in.

First I learned what the man wanted. He was crying, saying a mistake had been made. He never wanted to leave Cuba. He listened only to Fidel, the person he considered his father. He had a wife and child back home. He should not have been forced to leave.

He was so irrational I handled it in a manner I frequently used. I lied.

I told him I had a connection and would try to get him back. In the meantime, I persuaded him to be hospitalized in the psychiatric unit. I wrote up a report on the man, explaining that he had committed no crime in either country. I knew it would not work, but I also knew that we needed to keep each refugee's hope alive until the issue of their status could be resolved.

When I checked on the manic-depressive, I found the psychiatric ward ICU watch had placed him under wrist, ankle, and waist restraint, then injected him daily with the extreme tranquilizer Thorazine. I found that this same practice was used daily on the children who became frustrated, homesick, unruly, or tried to escape.

At other times I got called down by the FBI for saving people no one wanted saved. For example, one boy was cut severely, almost disemboweled, defending himself from a homosexual attack. He was found on the bathroom floor, defense lacerations on his hands and a gaping gut wound from a homemade machete. He was covered in blood and dying.

The single male population area was called the Boulevard. I had answered a radio call to the area. I ran into the barracks alone because my partner was unwilling to go in without backup. It went against procedure but I had no fear. The Cubans knew and trusted me.

The top joints of the victim's three fingers had been severed by the machete blade. I found them and placed them in a ziplock plastic bag, hoping they could be reattached. I compressed the gaping exposed intestines with sterile gauze from my first aid kit.

I had a boy go out and tell my partner to ready the hospital. I carried the youth and put him over my lap in the squad car. I thought he was going to die. He was able to tearfully speak, *"Marita, ayuda me, Santa Maria."* I ordered the driver to take the boy to Fort Smith where the hospital was better equipped to save his life and, possibly, reattach his fingers.

I got in trouble. The boy survived only because he was taken off base. To go off base in a Fort Chaffee vehicle was totally against policy. Without special authorization, which would have meant waiting longer than the boy could have survived, I was way out of line. I bucked the "system." As a result, I was dressed down by two FBI agents who called me a "fucking bleeding heart liberal Commie asshole." I thanked them for their concern. I was formally disciplined for ordering a military police vehicle off the base to take him from Fort Chaffee to Fort Smith.

The boy survived and wrote me letters of gratitude. He never should have been where he was. He was too young for the general male population barracks where he was attacked. He should have been in the unaccompanied children's area—a bureaucratic oversight.

The towns and communities around the camps were comfortable with the 125,000 refugees at first. The number of problem detainees was small compared with the majority with whom we were working. However, the trouble and the bad apples caused far exceeded their numbers. Many eventually wound up in federal prisons. For example, two men who were sponsored out and living in town killed a sheriff's deputy during a store robbery. Rapes, murders, armed robberies, and other violent crimes became commonplace. Because their actions were so often brutal and highly publicized, the thugs became the focus of community hostility, perpetuating the prejudice that they represented all the Cubans, and that everyone in the camp was a troublemaker waiting to happen.

There were thousands of acres of fenced land that formed the base. My son Mark, aged ten, joined me for breakfast in the mess hall at five A.M. Frequently I had to work twenty-four-hour shifts during disturbances, so chow was the only time we could be certain to be together until I returned to my apartment.

The Ku Klux Klan greatly influenced the local town surrounding the base. They hated the Cubans. There were regular cross burnings in areas visible to the base personnel. Mark and I felt that the community off the base was at times more hostile and threatening than the refugees at Fort Chaffee itself.

The Knights of the Ku Klux Klan of Metarie, Louisiana (Gene Furr, Area Organizer, and Mark Orsbun, Night Hawk) passed out a flyer that was acted out by the Fort Indiantown and then the Fort Chaffee clans.

1ST ANNUAL CUBAN SHOOT

TIME: 27 July 80 To 15 August 80

PLACE: Fort Indiantown Gap

LOCATION: Area 5

RULES: Open shoot, off-hand position only
NO SCOPES, NO SLINGS, NO TRIPODS
Open to all residents of Pennsylvania that pay taxes.
Those on welfare, ADC, Food stamps or any other giveaway are not eligible. (NOTE: do not complain about discrimination, your shoot will be announced later.)

SCORING: Pa. Rules apply; Point system will be utilized.

PLAIN CUBAN	5 points	
CUBAN WITH V.D.	10 points	Points may be added
CUBAN (FELON)	15 points	together for total
CUBAN (MURDERER) ..	25 points	scoring. Example:
CUBAN (SPY)	25 points	Cuban spy with V.D.
CUBAN (RUSSIAN SPY) .	50 points	worth 35 points.

JUDGES: Rev. Jesse Jackson   Vernon E. Jordan Jr. (if he lives)

PRIZES: Bags of peanuts and six packs of Billy Beer (donors may be on hand to autograph prizes)

SPONSOR: *Society Helping Individual Taxpayers Own Nothing* (known as SHIT ON)

ENTRY BLANK:

I _____ will attend the shoot. I plan on using _____ rounds of ammunition. Please reserve _____ cemetery lots for my trophies.

SIGNED _____

My apartment was off base in Arkansas. The chief of police lived close to us and looked out for Mark while I was on duty. I had to pay $20 in dues to the Klan, playing a double game to keep my son in grace. There were family picnics for the children on weekends. The children of Klan members had watermelon parties and hayrides. They also learned to shoot rifles so they could hunt and defend themselves.

Periodically a Cuban would escape over the fence before being sponsored out. If caught by the locals, he would be killed, his corpse dumped in the Arkansas River, or buried secretly. So I was told by Klan members who confided in me.

A high-ranking law enforcement officer in the community told me that his friends in the Klan were going to pitch Molotov cocktails onto the barracks. Because they were provided with disinformation by an insider, the barracks they firebombed were empty and no one was hurt. Had they been left to their own malicious devices, many lives could have been lost. Many more could have been injured.

There were Klan sympathizers among the guards and soldiers. A gun store in the area supplied cheap, small caliber arms that could be used to murder Cubans, then be tossed away. Arrangements were made to "lose" the paperwork on the victim. The person who was murdered just ceased to exist.

The single male Cuban population had an area in which to entertain themselves. The same was true for other detainees. The men could walk almost a mile for exercise within their authorized confinement area. There was a ballpark, a craft shop, music, and movies.

Most of the Cubans tried to make the best of their circumstances. There were pregnancies and births—children born U.S. citizens—including seven deliveries I assisted when the medics were delayed. Four baby girls were named Marita.

The refugees asked for seeds to grow a garden. They made handicrafts and other beautiful, highly inventive art work. They wrote letters to Castro, as well as to friends, relatives, and outside acquaintances. They made bootleg hootch for entertainment. Some painted sheets with slogans saying, FIDEL IS MY FATHER or I SHOULD HAVE LISTENED TO YOU. Then they hung the painted sheet out a window in protest.

Camp directors didn't want to have the newspeople see the sheets. I finally had to go into the barracks and tell the men that what they were doing was wonderful. It was "great art." It was very dramatic. I said I wanted them to do more, and instead of "wasting" the material by hanging it out the window, I suggested they hang it on the walls of the barracks. They agreed, never realizing that it was a compromise meant to prevent problems for everyone.

Many of the Cubans, particularly the younger ones, were amazed by the things they saw in the new land they now inhabited. They were fascinated by American music, clothes, sunglasses, cameras, audio equipment. They hoarded food because they had been deprived. They ate raw onions the way we eat apples. They had never seen snow. They had not celebrated Christmas the way we do. Everything was new, everything was thrilling to them.

I suspect that if anyone dug up the hillside outside the fort, a number of buried corpses would be found. It was not a pleasant part of our involvement with the detainees.

The saddest part of the detainees' story was the children. There were six hundred children, from infants to eighteen-year-olds, in detention. The children had been reared to believe in Fidel to such a degree that it was common to go by the barracks late at night and hear children crying out, "Fidel, help me!" There was boredom, neglect. There were almost no activities. Only one teacher was provided to help them adapt to U.S. ways and learn basic English-language skills. Beyond that they received no schooling.

For the teenagers there was an isolation area that was not much better than a jail cell. A teen who was upset was likely to be clubbed, restrained by hands and ankles, then injected with Thorazine. Since there were too few translators, it was often difficult to find someone such as myself who could talk a child through a crisis. They were homesick for Cuba, lost orphans, feeling hopeless and abandoned. They were scared of the unknown and afraid of the present. They needed someone to care about them, to love them, to help them adapt. Naturally some threw temper tantrums or acted their feelings out violently, like any normal child who has no other way to rebel or express himself. But unlike normal children, they would be clubbed and drugged as a result.

In one instance, a Federal officer took a pretty fifteen-year-old girl off base and into town. Some excuse was used, such as she needed special medical attention. However, once away from the base, she was raped. Eventually I discovered the pregnancy, helped the girl, and both she and her baby were sent to an orphanage in Atlanta. Later I learned that her child, a little girl, was named "Marita." I confronted the rapist and brought charges against him.

I stayed with the detention and relocation program for approximately eighteen months before returning to New York. I had learned much about present-day Cuba. The Cubans at the camps tended to be in good physical health, though deprived of many of the things we take for granted. They were literate. Many of them revered Fidel despite their deportation. But it was also obvious that he was a rigid ruler, willing to imprison young people for "crimes" no worse than a teen scribbling graffiti on a building wall. He demanded respect from the children for Cuba's future.

4

In September 1981, I returned to Cuba to see Fidel and meet our son.

At José Martí Airport they didn't know what to make of me. I wanted to speak with Fidel. I wanted to tell him what a lot of young Cuban boys said with their last breath at Fort Chaffee. Six of Fidel's G-2 officers and his cabinet interrogated me. My toughts were: "Kill me. Kill me. I'm going to get killed anyway by the CIA when I go back."

I told them over and over, "I want to speak to him personally. I don't want you to take notes. No, I don't work for anybody."

Six hours on that bench made me sore. I asked for water. A guard put his machine gun down, gave me a glass of water. I knew I was getting somewhere. He took a sip of the water first, then handed it to me. "Señora."

I could be coming back as an assassin twenty-two years later and I knew I could go to the wall. The minute I got the water, I knew I was safe.

I sat there about half an hour longer. The door opened. In stepped two more uniformed G-2 officers.

"Señora Lorenz? Come with us."

We drove through Havana. I saw the posters "Viva Che!" "Viva Camilo!" New highway. I smelled the *galande noche*, the jasmine.

We went through the *Védado* section. I remembered it from 1959. It was a nice treelined street, beautifully immaculate, scrupulously groomed, with little single houses, palm trees. One house had a satellite dish on top.

Two guards entered the house ahead of me, carrying my suitcase.

A fan is blowing to the right. An old man not in uniform comes to me as I'm walking in, takes my hand, kisses it, and bows down. He has one tooth missing. He holds my hand, squeezes it. He takes my other hand and squeezes that.

I look at him to see if I recognize him.

"Señora. Welcome to Cuba. Welcome home."

The guards brush him aside. They guide me to the left by the patio. An elegant house! Groomed gardens, beautiful woodwork, immaculate marble stairways, chandelier. Exquisite. I think "This must have been an old Batistiano" as I go up the staircase. As I reach the top, out comes a man from the far end of the hall wearing revolutionary uniform. He has a limp, perhaps a wooden leg, is middle-aged. About fifty. He greets me, but he doesn't smile. Nobody smiles. I shake hands with him. Instinctively, I snap my heels together in the style of Nazi Germany. It's not regulation U.S. Army attention salute. He picks that up. He looks at my feet. I smile with him.

I go straight through open doors into an immaculate room called *Casa Immigración*. It's got a double bed, white pillow cases, white sheets, night tables, shutters, windows. It's got an old-fashioned Cuban bathroom to the left with a bathtub, bidet.

There's a dresser with an ashtray. In the ashtray is a half-smoked cigar. The lights are turned low.

"Do you wish to have a guard?" I turn to the man.

"From what? From whom? I'm in Cuba. I'm not afraid."

My suitcases are put down. Two guards come in and sit on two chairs.

It's a pretty large room. I sit on the edge of the bed. The shutters are closed. The phone line is pulled out.

"Would you like to freshen up?"

"Yes." I go into the bathroom. The bidet is a whole room in itself. I see little Russian soaps, little cheap towels. This kid—he's about 27—with his AK-47 follows me into the bathroom.

I open the shutters in the bathroom. He closes them. I open them again. I walk back into the bedroom.

"I want these open."

"No. The Russians are down the street."

"Look, I don't care who's down the street. I'm in Cuba. I'm happy. I want to smell the air, so please leave the window open. Okay?"

I'm pacing. I picked up Fidel's habit of pacing back and forth.

"Where's the chief? I know he's never prompt. But I want to see him!"

All of a sudden I hear a rock song coming from a distance. I think I'm in spaceland. I try the doors.

"Who's got the gringo music?"

The guard waves me off.

I go back to the bathroom. I take a shower, wash my face, put on new makeup, and think "To hell with it if Fidel walks in and I don't have my makeup on. He owes me his life anyway." I cop this attitude to condition myself. I don't know what will happen. Maybe they're going to let me clean up before they put me before the firing squad. There's always that chance.

I freshen up and I sit on the bed. Then, the twisted official with the limp comes in bringing me paper, really crummy Russian paper, and a pencil.

"Write."

"Write what?"

"Anything."

"No. I want to see Fidel. If I want to write him a letter I can do that from the United States. I want to see him now! What I have to say, I have to say in person."

"Yes. He's coming."

When he said that, everything changed. I calmed down.

"I have your passport. It's safe with me. You will get it back."

"Fine. You want to search me? In my pocket I have $10,000 in cash. You want the money?" I put it on the table. "Here. $10,000."

"No. No. No."

I wanted them to trust me. I went over to the ashtray with the half-smoked cigar. I turned to the soldiers inside the room.

"What's your name?"

"Carlos."

"Do you smoke cigars?" He lit up like a Christmas tree.

"No, *El Hefe* does."

"In the United States, in an interview Fidel said he's giving up smoking because it was bad for his health. But he still smokes?"

"Sí, but for the public he smokes the little cigars. He cut down on the big cigars."

Steps. They jump to attention. Put their rifles right next to them.

I could smell his familiar stogie before they opened the door. I sat on the edge of the bed straight, right in front of the door. The minute he walked in—I don't know what it is, my military training, I don't know what—I stood up. He stopped cold, dead in his tracks. I looked at him. He looked at me, stared at me.

Fidel turned to the guards. "It's okay." They turned to go out.

I sat back down. I said nothing. I couldn't find words. I mean, I'm back after the assassination try. I really did not believe that he would see me. I really didn't believe it. But I put on such a stink at the airport demanding this and that. He stood in that door twenty-two years later, put his hand down, flicked his cigar on the floor and stared at me. He looked at me with no expression. The guards with their AK-47s left saluting, "Sí comandante. Sí comandante."

Fidel shut the door behind them and looked at me. He looked just about the same: a little more gray, a little heavier around the gut. Still a sidearm, probably the same, old rusty .45 he handed me twenty-two years ago. It didn't work then. Probably didn't work now. I was happy, relieved, a little nervous, but I had to recharge my batteries to start my tirade all over again with him. I wanted to explain to him personally what happened at Fort Chaffee.

"Been a long time. I've missed you many years." I wanted to be neutral. I didn't know what else to say.

Fidel walked to the right, looked around, walked back to me, extended his hand. By this time, I stood up by the edge of the bed. He gave me a dry, firm handshake, but didn't let go of my hand.

"Welcome back, my little assassin."

I just grinned. He laughed. I saw that space. It was something I noticed when I was with him in '59. He needed a filling between the front teeth. He got that fixed. It's the weirdest thing, but that's what I noticed first. His teeth were perfect, bonded, no dentures, his smile brilliant. We both said nothing, both laughed again.

I looked at him. Without a word at that same split-second, we hugged each other. The woman in me wanted to cry. The same familiar hug.

"Too much time, Fidel."

"You're still alive."

"Yes, you, too. Thanks to me."

"Yes. I know, I know."

He didn't know what to say. I didn't know what to say. I picked myself up and I tried to be that hateful person with Chaffee memories boiling inside. But all of a sudden I was back in 1959. His face was inches from mine.

"Fidel, you owe me." I didn't know the Spanish word for "owe."

"What did you say?" Then he hugged me again. I felt I should push him away.

"It's been a long time, Fidel."

"Yes, both of us were very young."

"And my reputation is ruined because of you."

He took me by the shoulders. "What about you? What about you? You went with Pérez-Jiménez, had an affair with Pérez-Jiménez! He's bald, fat, and ugly. And you had a child by him."

He caught me off guard with that. "Don't talk to me about Pérez-Jiménez." He turned away from me, turned his back on me.

"Yes! I had a child by him!" I answered. "But I *have* that child. Where is mine with you? I didn't come here to talk to you about my romance and your romance. He turned around and walked to the window.

"I can take anything except your affair with Pérez-Jiménez."

"Fidel, I loved you. I still love you, I guess. But have you

246

any idea of what a real pain-in-the-ass you have been in my life? I was stigmatized, a pawn of the government of the United States. Do you think it was easy for me to raise two children?"

"TWO!"

"Two. One by Pérez-Jiménez, one by someone you don't have to know about. A boy. I'm not here to talk about your personal life or mine. I'm here for another reason. Number one, I think you look pretty good and I'm divorced. Maybe I'll come back to stay."

"Are you going to stay here?"

"Fidel, I have two children in the United States. I'm here, one, to tell you about my private little war with your *gusanos*. I'm not here representing anyone. I'm me. I do not represent any intelligence agency."

"I hope not."

"I'll probably get killed when I get back, because I know the CIA knows I'm here."

"You don't have to return. You stay here!"

"I came here because President Carter lifted travel restrictions. . . ."

"He's a good man. I like him. I liked Kennedy. I like Carter."

I was trying to build myself up to fire at him. I had to find the words. Meanwhile, he paced back and forth.

"You still smoke the big cigar. The New York papers said you quit smoking."

"That's your American press.

In the middle of all this he said, "You still look pretty good."

"Well, your little assassin came back. You may kill me if you like."

"No! No. Why did you come?"

"Maybe I came here to kill you. Maybe I got a little fix of

three million dollars and I'm here to kill you. Your men didn't open my bag."

"You can't do that. You won't do that."

"You haven't changed, Fidel. You're still arrogant! And I'm proud of your achievements for Cuba."

I composed myself and sat down on the bed. "Do you know why I came here, Fidel? Because for the last two years you have been in my mind, every goddam day. Because I was in the army taking care of your *Marielitos*."

I pulled out my Unlimited Access identification card from Fort Chaffee. "You can shoot me after this. But I'm not gonna shut up. My heart so weeps for the ones who died."

"What happened?"

"Why did you overwhelm the U.S. with this many?"

"I have a shortage of food, overcrowded prisons. I couldn't care for them all."

"Fidel, there were six hundred children. . . ."

"Children of dissidents. Children that weren't wanted. Children I couldn't feed."

"Okay. I'll buy that. Have you any idea what happened to them over there?" His eyes got real wide. He sat on the side of the bed next to me and held my hand.

"Tell me."

"Do you know how many suicides were calling your name at the end? Do you know this camp cost the Americans two million dollars a day? Do you know of those that have been murdered because of their color?" He kept his head down, they slowly looked up to me, eyes questioning, his face very close to mine.

"I came here to scream at you. But I'm tired. I already told your men the same thing. They gave me a pad and pencil, but I can't put it on paper, because my heart fills with so much pain. I really have no right to tell you this. But I want you to suffer the way I suffered. I want you to suffer with the little boys that called for you with their last breath while I held them in my arms. 'Tell Fidel I love him.' I want to give you this bedsheet written in blood by a sixteen-year-old who hung himself. I want to give you this personnally. It's addressed to you. From one of your lost *gusanos*. I'm really so tired. It's three in the morning. I've been up since six yesterday morning. I really wanted to scream at you. I wanted to hit you. I want you to have the tears in your eyes that I had in mine for two years. They were bad Cubans. They were good Cubans. But they were all of Cuban blood. There were six hundred orphans, single males, families. They were your Cubans, Fidel! What's wrong here in Cuba that you sent so many?"

He stood up.

"They wanted to leave, I let them go."

"I don't know if you made a mistake. I just want to tell you the words I remember of many, many children. I want to tell you of the little boys who were shot. I want to tell you of the abuse. You're never gonna hear it from anywhere else."

"Would you want to talk to my Cabinet?"

"Fuck that. You're Cuba, goddamn it!" He looked at me, held my hand.

"Bring your children. You have a house. You have everything."

"They won't come now. They're too old now to come willingly, except for a visit. Fidel, I have *another* little boy, who I didn't nurse, here with you. Could you tell me about him now? I would like to know, Fidel. There's a big hole in my heart. My mother died in '77. She was corresponding with you. She left me a picture of a little boy, who looks just like you and me. What happened to that child?"

Fidel stood up and started pacing. He got defensive. He couldn't light the match, so I gave him my lighter. He lit the

249

stump of his cigar. "Take a deep breath and tell me. Our boy. My blood. Your blood."

"All children born in Cuba belong to the father."

"That's not an answer. That's your revolutionary law. Those children each had a mother!" Then, he started to clench his fist. I thought, Oh shit, I'm going too far.

"I want to see this boy. Is he alive? Please, please Fidel?"

"He's not yours. He's not yours. He belongs to Cuba."

"Can I just see him? Or do I have to start an international incident. You can put me to the wall tomorrow. I want to know if he's alive and well."

"Yes! He's alive and well."

"Okay. All I want is to see my son. I want to see him, Fidel, I have that right as a mother."

"You have two other children. You don't need this one."

He's getting temperamental and walking toward the door. I grab him, put my arms around his waist. He's six-foot-three. I've got on sneakers, jeans, a white blouse and navy blazer. I tug his gun belt.

"Fidel, please. Just tell me." I started crying.

"Marita, there is no way I will let you take my child out of the country."

"*Fidel, there is no way* I *intend* to take our child to the United States. *I know better.* I just have to see him. Just let me see him once and I'll leave."

Fidel doesn't answer. He's good at that. He walks to the French doors, opens the shutters, walks out on the balcony, puffs his cigar. I follow him out.

"I'm a woman. I'm a mother. I saved your life. I just want a trade. Just let me see my son and I'll never bother you again. I'm sorry I can't stop the press in America from writing about us. It is out and that's the way of the American press. I despise it."

Fidel says nothing. He is thinking, stretching.

"Why are the streetlights so low?"

"Anytime there will be an invasion from your people, your CIA."

"No, they are not my people. I wasn't born in the United States."

"You worked with the CIA. You betrayed your homeland, Germany."

"Fidel, it's very hard for me to explain to you now. I have a child, a daughter, a very beautiful daughter. I have a letter from her, because you denied her an entry visa. She was packed and ready to go. And she really hates you for that."

"Tell her I'm sorry. I just didn't want problems from Pérez-Jiménez."

"Fuck him. He doesn't care about his daughter. Monica admires you. And she wrote you this letter in her own handwriting." I take it out of my vest pocket, rip open the sealed envelope, marked "personal to Fidel Castro." I read it as we stand on the balcony.

Dear Fidel,
    You really piss me off. I hate you for not permitting me to go on this trip to Cuba. I hope you read this and do not condemn me for who my father is. I respect and admire you and I have a brother somewhere in Cuba. I think you stink for not giving me a visa. Please reconsider.
    I love you,
    Monica

Fidel just looks ahead.

"I like the smell of the jasmine," I say, giving him the letter. He puts his arm around my waist. I put my head on his shoulder.

"Please, Fidel."

"I need a coffee." Fidel squeezes my waist. "We have no coffee."

"Fidel, Cuba is not Cuba without Cuban coffee."

"Marita, the old man downstairs will tell you about the son."

"Our son."

"He's fine. He's fine. But he is mine."

"All right. I would like to see him one time. I will make no demands, have no further contact. Let me see him."

He turns me around again with his hands on my shoulders and hugs me. "One look. I will let you meet the boy. He's a good boy. He's a doctor. You'll be proud of him."

"He's a doctor?" I started to cry. "What kind?"

"Baby doctor."

"Something I always wanted to be." Right away I think he's got my genes.

"He's a good boy. And the old man you met downstairs is the one who raised him."

"Just a few minutes." He leaves the door open, walks to the door next to the porch, calls, "Andre!"

I think: "Andre?"

My first glance is of a tall young boy: white skin, black curly hair. Fidel's nose, my mouth, my eyes. He is zipping up and belting his pants. Cloth shoes. Simple shirt, no jewelry, no watch.

"I want you to see somebody."

Here I am, feeling small. I see this young man and I see me and Fidel. He seems kind of annoyed at Fidel for disturbing him. I try to stand up straight. I look at him again and the tears start running.

Fidel shuts the door behind him and gestures at me as if to say, "There she is."

The boy straightens up and very politely takes my hand.

"How do you do? "Then, Oh Señora, don't cry. Why are you crying?"

I don't think he knows.

I just hug him.

He is distant as if he is thinking: "Why is this crazy woman hugging me?"

Fidel walks away, fiddles with the ashtray, then walks back to us and says: "That's your real mother."

Andre stops cold. The distance between us melts.

"May I call you Mother?"

"Yes. I just wanted to see you. Your Poppa let me see you. I don't want to disrupt your life. I just want to see you one time."

"Oh yes Poppa told me before. I'm happy to meet you."

"I wasn't a good mother. I . . . wasn't here . . . they took . . ."

"Don't worry! Everything is fine. I'm a good boy!"

"I never saw you. I never changed your diapers. I never nursed you. I never cradled you. I was taken away drugged. I thought you were dead. I have two more children, a little boy and a very pretty little girl."

"Oh yes! Really?"

I look at Andre and hold his face in my hands.

Fidel's looking out the window. He's taking every word in.

I want to look at his hands to see if they're like mine. I want to examine him. I'm in total awe. I say, "I'm very proud of you. What more can I say?"

"Nothing! Nothing. You know I'm happy to meet you. Poppa told me about you. But you know I have other parents. The old man downstairs was a professor at school. I'm not military, you know. I'm a doctor. I want to save lives. I'm very proud of my studies. Poppa is too."

I sit down on the bed.

253

"Can I give you anything? I'm trying to make up for the lack of motherhood. I have to give you something."

"No. You don't have to. I have everything."

I have brought him a tape recorder and a Polaroid camera, blue jeans, three pairs of sneakers.

I open the suitcase. As soon as Fidel sees the Polaroid, he can't resist it.

That's the way it goes. The tape recorder, tapes, jeans, the Polaroid, the eighteen cases of Polaroid film. All three of us go through everything.

I give Andre the tape recorder to help with his studies. Fidel says: "Okay he gets the tape recorder and I get the camera." Like two kids.

DOCUMENTS

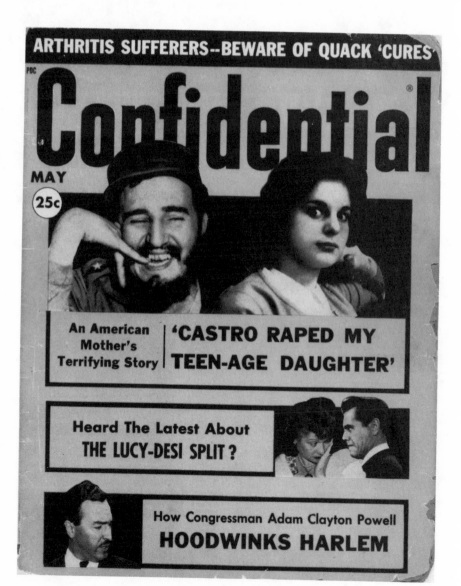

ARTHRITIS SUFFERERS--BEWARE OF QUACK 'CURES'

PDC

Confidential ®

MAY

25c

An American Mother's Terrifying Story | 'CASTRO RAPED MY TEEN-AGE DAUGHTER'

Heard The Latest About THE LUCY-DESI SPLIT?

How Congressman Adam Clayton Powell HOODWINKS HARLEM

„Vieles, was über mich geschrieben wurde, ist falsch, weil keiner bisher mit mir gesprochen hatte." Das sagt die 35jährige attraktive Ilona-Marita Lorenz, die jahrelang die Geliebte des kubanischen Diktators Fidel Castro war und ihn im Auftrag des US-Geheimdienstes CIA ausspionierte. Exklusiv für BILD am SONN-TAG berichtet sie über ihr gefährliches Leben.

So liebte ich Fidel Castro

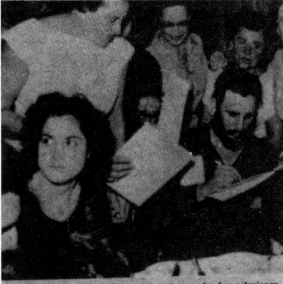

FIDEL with Marita (left), signs autographs for admirers.

Erstes Treffen am 28. Februar 1959. Marita sitzt neben Castro. Rechts Maritas Vater, Kapitän des Passagierschiffes „Berlin"

W'GATE BURGLAR ARRESTED HERE

Cover Blown By Sturgis — "Refusing Angola Assignment"

By JOSEPH P. COTTER and MEL JUFFE

Carey media whiz may bolt

Page 2

Watergate burglar Frank Sturgis was arrested here late last night for allegedly threatening an upper East Side woman who has linked Sturgis to the assassination of President Kennedy.

The woman is Marita Lorenz of 512 E. 88th St., a former CIA spy who reportedly once lived with Cuban Premier Fidel Castro as Castro's lover.

Sturgis was arrested by Police Dept. intelligence detectives in Miss Lorenz's apartment at 11:30 last night and was to be arraigned today on felony charges of coercion in Manhattan Criminal Court.

Miss Lorenz last Saturday told House Assassinations Committee investigators in an interview about a trip she said she took with Oswald, Sturgis and four others—all members of an assassination squad. She said that they arrived in Dallas Nov. 19, three days before the murder of President Kennedy in 1963.

Sturgis and Miss Lorenz also have said that Sturgis

one assigned to—in 1960—to kill Castro.

Police said Sturgis how heard and reached interval

Frank Sturgis and Marita Lorenz last year.

Superspy Marita tells her story

Photo by Jean Michel/Liaison

Marita's 15-year-old daughter Monica stands beside a photograph of her father, Perez Jiménez, former Venezuelan dictator.

Continued from Page 1

daughter for protecting me," she said from her luxury apartment on East 88th Street.

POLICE GUARD

She made the statement while holed up with five detectives, two of them armed with shotguns.

The detectives have barred reporters from the building, refuse to take her out to eat and taste test food that is ordered in from outside.

In a disjoined talk, Miss Lorenz said, she had not slept for two days and was exhausted but added: "Between the police, my daughter and the way I can handle myself, I have good protection.

The daughter's father is former Venezuelan dictator Marcos Perez Jiminez.

"All I want now is a little bottle of Chablis wine to relax with," Mrs. Lorenz said. She insisted at the suggestion she was working through a lawyer to sell her memoirs.

"What lawyer? I have no lawyer." She appeared annoyed at the talk of money. "I don't need money. You keep it, you need it."

WORKED ON BOOK

Despite her denials that she is interested in money or publication of books, she has worked on her memoirs with two authors in the past 18 months.

And she confirmed that if she did write a book, it would be sizzling.

"Love letters from Castro," she said, then perhaps, realizing she might be breaking orders to keep silent, added: "I can't talk. I can't say anything."

Miss Lorenz, who has claimed in the past that she is a crack pistol shot, was Fidel Castro's mistress for eight months.

After being recruited by Sturgis for the assassination of Castro, she landed in Havana with a loaded gun.

"And believe me, I know how to use it and wouldn't hesitate to use it if I have to."

MISSION FAILED

Miss Lorenz added that her assassination attempt, which failed when poison capsules melted in some cold cream in which they were concealed, almost cost her life.

She said two armed Cubans to tried to pistol whip her and kidnap her from a telephone booth on East 60th Street in March of 1960. They fled when a passerby approached.

"Since then I always have made sure that I have had access to a gun," she said.

During conversation with The Post last night one of the shotgun-toting detectives forcibly ejected a TV re-

porter who had got into the apartment.

Meanwhile, Miss Lorenz is scheduled to face a grand jury in connection with her allegations that Sturgis had threatened her.

GRAND JURY PROBE

At his arraignment, the District Attorney's office charged that Sturgis instilled "fear into her that she would be killed," if she continued to talk to investigators of the subcommittee about the Kennedy assassination.

They claimed that Sturgis had threatened that he or someone else would harm her or "the Company would get her." The word company is a reference to the CIA.

Henry Rothblatt, Sturgis' lawyer, in an attempt to lower the unusually high bail of $25,000, said that Miss Lorenz's charge stemmed from the fact she was writing a book and was searching for publicity.

Miss Lorenz has claimed in testimony that she. Sturgis and Lee Harvey Oswald were among seven people who traveled from Miami to Dallas as part of an assassination squad.

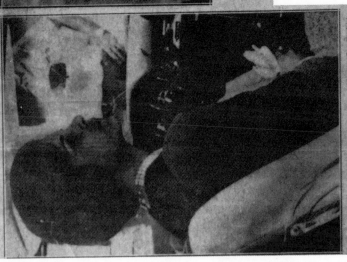

He's Losing
His Appeal

Marcos Perez Jimenez, (white shirt), former dictator of Venezuela, smiles with tight lips as U.S. and Venezuelan security officers escort him to plane in Miami. He was fresh out of court appeals to keep him in the U.S. Daughter, Margot, 17, (foto right), grieves at his departure: American husband comforts her. Jimenez will await embezzlement charges in an air-conditioned cell. Marita Lorenz (foto left), filed faternity suit against him.

(UPI Telefoto)

Marita Lorenz, at Miami Airport, watches Jimenez' plane leave.

(Associated Press Wirefoto)

Asks U.S. Guard Spy In Castro Death Plot

By PAUL MESKIL

A member of the Senate Intelligence Committee has requested Justice Department protection for Marita Lorenz, the shapely spy who told the panel she had been recruited in 1960 by the CIA to kill her former lover, Fidel Castro.

The request was made by Sen. Richard Schweiker (R-Pa.) after Ms. Lorenz allegedly was pistol-whipped in her Manhattan apartment last month, The News learned yesterday.

Ms. Lorenz said her attacker threatened to kill her and her two children. She said he later phoned her apartment building and told the superintendent Ms. Lorenz would "get what Roselli got," an apparent reference to Mafia don John Roselli, whose body was found Aug. 7 in an oil drum floating in a Miami waterway.

Roselli had participated in CIA plots to assassinate Castro. Ms. Lorenz said the threatening phone call came hours after Roselli's body was found.

No Reply

On Aug. 13, two days after Ms. Lorenz' alleged assailant was arrested here, Schweiker sent a letter to U.S. Attorney General Edward Levi, requesting protection for her. He has not yet received a reply.

A Levi spokesman said the attorney general "referred the letter to the criminal Division for review. It is still under review."

Meanwhile, Ms. Lorenz, her teenage daughter and small son are living behind locked doors in their East Side apartment. The E. 102d St. police precinct has been guarding her residence since the attack, but is unable to provide round-the-clock protection because of the manpower shortage.

Ms. Lorenz said she worked as an undercover agent for the CIA in the early 1960s and thereafter, for about 15 years, performed similar work for the FBI. But the New York office of the FBI has ignored her pleas for protection she charged.

FBI Commendation

In 1971 she received an FBI commendation from John F. Malone, who was then in charge of the New York office. Written on an FBI letterhead and marked "personal and confidential," Malone's note said in part:

"It has recently been brought to my attention that assistance being given by you has been of extreme value to the United States Government and the

Marita Lorenz
Receives death threats

operation of this bureau in particular.

"Your cooperation, devotion and sincerity are most appreciated by this bureau and matters of a security and criminal nature are now being handled in a more thorough manner because of your unselfish desire to assist."

The citation was for her undivulged help in a national security probe in 1971.

Ms. Lorenz said she was working on an organized crime investigation recently for the FBI when she became involved with the man who allegedly attacked and threatened her.

Police identified him as Giuseppe Fagiano, 1406 W. Sixth St., Brooklyn. According to a police report on the attack, she was beaten on the head, face and body with a gun. She later was treated at Mount Sinai Hospital.

Fagiano was arrested Aug. 11 for first-degree assault, possession of a dangerous weapon and aggravated harassment. Arraigned in Manhattan Criminal Court, he was released on his own recognizance pending a hearing tomorrow. Ms. Lorenz said the anonymous telephone threats on her life have continued since Fagiano was released.

Women shy over JFK slay book

By FRANK DiGIACOMO and
JOANNA MOLLOY
With Florence Anthony

VETERAN Kennedy assassination conspiracy theorist Mark Lane is raring to prove with his new book that the CIA killed JFK — but some of the tome's pivotal characters aren't so eager.

"Thunder's Mouth Press, publisher of "Plausible Denial," has had to hire two private detectives to track down two women who play key roles in the book, and convince them to participate in the tome's P.R. campaign.

"Plausible Denial," due out on the 18th anniversary of JFK's murder, focuses on a 1985 libel trial that overturned an award against a writer who claimed that Watergate burglar and former CIA agent E. Howard Hunt might have had a role in the crime.

Although both women were located, one — a former CIA operative who's the mother of Cuba leader Fidel Castro's child — wants to keep her whereabouts a secret. Former superspy Marita Lorenz — whose identity was pre-

viously concealed by the publisher and author — agreed to appear in a 40-minute videotaped interview that Lane has already shot, but otherwise will keep a low profile. "She doesn't want anyone to find her," says Lane.

During the 1985 trial, Lane explains, Lorenz gave key testimony — also videotaped — that placed Hunt in Dallas days before the assassination with a group of people, one of whom subsequently admitted to her he'd been involved in the crime.

In 1977, Lorenz reportedly accused her old espionage partner, Watergate burglar Frank Sturgis, of threatening her if she continued to talk to authorities about the assassination. Sturgis was arrested but acquitted.

Earlier in her colorful life, Lorenz not only had an eight-month affair and a child with Castro but also reportedly was recruited by Sturgis for a failed mission to kill the hirsute Havana honcho.

After nearly six weeks of searching, a detective also found Leslie Armstrong, running a help-oriented talk show for substance abusers on a Miami radio station.

Armstrong, who was the jury forewoman in the libel case, had moved from her Florida home without leaving a forwarding address. "When I first got wind that they were fishing around for me, I was not responsive," Armstrong told us in a phone interview. "I figured it was the CIA."

When Armstrong realized it was Lane who was seeking her, she agreed to cooperate and has even provided this statement for the publisher to release: "Mr. Lane was asking us [the jury] to do something very difficult — he was asking us to believe that John Kennedy had been killed by our own government. Yet when we examined the evidence closely, we were compelled to conclude that the CIA had indeed killed President Kennedy."

INDEX

263